TURNABOUT

TURNABOUT

Stories of individuals who overcame tough
challenges to move from dependency to self-
sufficiency in this amazing country of ours — and
the lessons we can learn from them.

Peter Heegaard

NODIN PRESS

ISBN: 978-1-935666-79-0

We gratefully acknowledge the support of the Urban Adventure Funds of both the Minneapolis Foundation and the Greater Twin Cities United Way.

Royalties received by the author that exceed expenses will be donated to the non-profits featured in this book.

Cover photos: upper right © Hongqi Zhang (aka Michael Zhang) | Dreamstime.com; lower left Stock photo © Primeop76; lower right courtesy of Advocates for Human Rights.

Library of Congress Cataloging-in-Publication Data

Heegaard, Peter A.
  Turnabout : stories of individuals who overcame tough challenges to move from dependency to self-sufficiency in this amazing country of ours--and the lessons we can learn from them / Peter Heegaard.
    pages cm
  ISBN 978-1-935666-79-0
  1. Community development--United States--Case studies. 2. Voluntarism--United States--Case studies. 3. Social service--United States--Case studies. 4. Success--United States--Case studies. 5. Self-reliance--United States--Case studies. 6. Nonprofit organizations--United States. I. Title.
  HN90.C6H44 2015
  302'.14--dc23
                                    2015005552

Nodin Press, LLC
5114 Cedar Lake Road
Minneapolis, MN
55416

*This book is dedicated to my grandchildren
in hopes that they will experience many of the same rewards
that their grandmother and I have enjoyed
in being actively involved in civic engagement and
community building.
For Sara, Ned, Thomas, Annie, John, Emily,
Ellie, and Peter*

Contents

Introduction   1

David Ellis   5

A disruptive African American teen developed a teaching style and a high school that gives some of our most challenged teenagers a new lease on life.

Bibi Abdalla   20

This Kenyan girl struggled to relate to the culture of her parents while learning a new language and trying to be accepted into the culture of a new world.

Kandy McDonal   30

A single mom from an unstable family held down a job while navigating the support systems so that her children could be educated in quality pre-K schools.

Pa Kong Lee   38

Coming from a refugee camp in Southeast Asia to the Twin Cities, Pa Kong Lee can look forward to college because of a program created by a young social entrepreneur.

John Turnipseed   45

A middle-aged African American, once part of one of the region's most notorious crime families, turns his life around to help fatherless boys find meaning in their lives.

Ashley Bath   64

She survived a perfect storm of abuse, neglect, homelessness and drug abuse, with help from a no-nonsense grandmother and a caring workforce counselor.

Cherkos Dessalegn   73

Arriving from Ethiopia at age fifteen, he excelled at school, attended college, and found work giving students the mentoring and encouragement he never received.

Beth Milbrandt   83

After years of loneliness on the reservation, drug abuse, and federal prison, she developed leadership skills and found rewarding work through an excellent work force training program.

Shegitu Kebede 89

She endured painful degradations as a refugee but has
overcome the worst and is now experiencing the best as a
restaurant owner and community leader.

Raymond Jackson 100

Suffering brutal child abuse and an early life in criminal activities,
this young man benefited from an outstanding rehabilitation
program and says at age thirty-two, "for the first time I feel loved."

Ibro Tabakovic 106

Ethnic cleansing in Serbia forced this college president and his
family to flee their homeland. Coming to America, he distinguished
himself by advancing technology in computer science.

Lante Morris 118

He made good money selling crack, but he wasn't aware of the risk.
His slide into crime and later rehabilitation offer insights into the
types of programs that actually lower the recidivism rate.

John Pacheco 127

This story takes us from a youth detention facility to leadership
positions in several non-profit organizations and an executive
position in a Fortune 500 Company.

Tiffany Meeks 137

A single mom, age nineteen, she learned of a non-profit founded by
a remarkable priest that provided day care, housing, and counseling
so that she could find work at a livable wage.

Epilogue 142

Further Information About the Organizations 147

Acknowledgments 176

Further information about the organizations referred to in these stories

The Advocates for Human Rights 147

African Development Center 148

Better Futures Minnesota 149

The Center for Victims of Torture 151

The City, Inc. 152

City of Lakes Community Land Trust 153

College Possible 154

Common Bond Communities 156

High School for Recording Arts 158

Hired 158

Jeremiah 160

The Legal Rights Center 162

Local Initiatives Support Corporation 163

Lutheran Social Services 164

The Minneapolis Urban Coalition 165

Neighborhood Development Center 166

Summit Academy OIC 167

Think Small 169

Twin Cities Rise! 171

Ujamaa Place 172

Urban Ventures Leadership Foundation 173

Introduction

What follows are stories about people who overcame extremely tough challenges to achieve the American Dream. Some of them are about new immigrants who faced extreme violence early in life and are now political refugees. Others relate to generational poverty shared by individuals coming from dysfunctional families with no positive role models. Included are stories by young people from stable working class families who, either through boredom or peer pressure, became involved in gang related activities and ended up in prison. Each of these stories involve people who have struggled and overcome adversity with the help of others to become contributing members of society, and sometimes executives and entrepreneurs.

I'm curious about how these people moved from dependency to self-sufficiency in this amazing country of ours. I'm curious about how new immigrants and refugees who have left everything behind in their native lands acclimate to a new life in America, and how families with a history of unemployment and reliance on welfare break with their past and become self-sufficient. Have we learned how to help those whose lives have been managed by the criminal justice system stay out of prison and become productive members of society? Is it possible for people with minimum-wage jobs to gain new skills or become entrepreneurs? Why are our prisons so disproportionally filled with people of color, especially young African American males?

How does racism impact the ability of individuals and families to realize the American Dream? In general, which programs work and which do not?

By listening carefully to the stories contained in this book, alert to the elements that helped the individuals involved to succeed, we may begin to get answers to some of these questions. We know that the system fails many of our less fortunate individuals and families due to chronic poverty, abuse and neglect, racism, lack of a good education, and a host of other factors. The good news is that for the most part we now know what works. The right individual intervening at the right moment can turn a person's life around. Where do these social helpers come from, and how do they learn when and how to intervene? The challenge is to connect the dots in our communities so that more people can help others become contributing members of society.

My wife, Anne, and I have been involved in a wide range of non-profit organizations for more than fifty years. Most of them are supported by individual and corporate philanthropy, though some receive government support. We have watched some organizations thrive while others serve their time and disappear, just as businesses and corporations do. Much of our spare time over the years has been devoted either to serving such programs or educating others about them.

My first book, *Heroes Among Us*, describes individuals who started non-profits and built them up to where they became preeminent in their field. Many of these "social entrepreneurs" started their careers in the private sector, but somewhere along the way something happened that caused them to change course. They chose to work for less money in the non-profit sector but earned more life satisfaction in the process. My second book, *More Bang for Your Buck*, applied many of the financial metrics used in my former life as an investment advisor and security analyst to non-profit organizations. It documents the fact that many non-profits not only help families and communities but also save tax dollars. In this new book, I've gathered stories of a few individuals who have been helped by non-profit organizations—or by the "independent sector," as it's sometimes called—and are now contributing members of our community.

The process for pulling these stories together involved securing nominations from community leaders whom my wife and I have known for many years, including many through an urban education program I teach to business executives called Urban Adventure. There was first a phone call to the prospective story-teller, explaining who I am and the purpose of the book. Then I took a deep breath and asked if they would be willing to be interviewed. Fortunately, in most cases the answer was yes! We met, and with the tape recorder running I conducted the interview. Once the interview was transcribed, the interviewee made appropriate changes, and I added background comments, which are printed here in bold lettering.

What I found most fascinating about the process was the joy and enthusiasm that developed as individuals told their stories. I felt as though I were there with them as they described the hardships they endured and their road to recovery. I hope you'll experience the same feelings as you read the text. The stories are hopeful and inspiring. They reaffirm that we do have the tools and the know-how to keep the American dream alive for years to come.

The people in my home state of Minnesota have a solid record of volunteerism and service to their neighbors. Corporations, foundations, and government have enthusiastically supported programs that help individuals and families achieve self-sufficiency. The good news, as I mentioned earlier, is that for the most part we now know what works to make our communities healthier and economically more supportive for all citizens. The challenge lies in creating the willingness to allocate sufficient human and financial resources to get the job done.

David Ellis

"Who says you can't be a successful metal worker or carpenter or chef? Many of these kids simply don't have the means to finance a college education. You have to remember that for many of these kids the starting point was teaching them how to cope and survive."

One of the highlights of the past year for me was listening to Dave Ellis describe his troubled school years and how that experience caused him to invent a teaching style that has given some of our most challenged teenagers a new lease on life. He is a master at applying tactile learning techniques to the areas of interest that turn students on. In his case that was music, and more specifically rap and hip hop. By meeting students where they were in terms of their interest in the arts, he not only dramatically improved their odds of graduating from high school but also positioned them well for the world of work.

Thanks for letting me share my story. My earliest memories of my family are pretty great. I was born and raised in the heart of the Summit/University area of St. Paul, Minnesota. Our home was at Fuller and Milton. My father was a railroad waiter on the Empire Builder, and my mother was a housewife who later on did domestic work for the family of J. C. Duke, an executive at 3M Company. Mr. Duke used to tell me stories about when 3M got its first airplane back in the 1930s.

I went to kindergarten at Maxfield Elementary, and then I was sent to St. Peter Claiborne, a Catholic school. That's where the shenanigans started. It was a very rigid strict academic environment, and I wasn't cut out for that learning style. I preferred an "outside the box," left-brain, free-spirited approach. My learning style is experiential—I have to be involved in things to really understand them. If you merely tell me something I may forget it, but if I can touch and feel how something works, it will stay with me.

I failed the second grade at St. Peter Claiborne. That was the beginning of my resistance to a traditional classroom environment. Then I became part of the original busing movement they developed in that community; I was among the first group of inner city kids bussed from that area out to Highland Park. The pattern was much the same in third grade as I was identified as having learning disabilities and was even prescribed some medicine. The only other black kid in that school with me—his name was Ronnie—experienced the same thing. Right before lunch we'd have to go to the nurse's office to get our daily pills. Ronnie explained to me how he would put the stuff under his tongue, drink the water, and go to the bathroom afterwards to spit the medicine out. So I started doing the same thing. That was about 1968.

The two of us got into trouble there repeatedly, though once we got into fifth and sixth grades some of the teachers tried harder to relate to us. Both Mrs. Mahon and Mrs. Rock were incredible teachers. They created special projects for me and came up with assignments outside the normal curriculum. Somehow they had spotted my nervousness and anxiety.

In fifth grade I participated in a program called Talking Typewriter—even on Saturday! A primitive computer would ask you questions, you'd type in the answers, and the words would appear on the screen. I gravitated towards that program because it was interactive. It helped me catch up on my reading and writing.

My experience in middle school at Highland Park was also a trial, although anything to do with metal working or woodworking held my interest, and I also did well in music. I could not read music, but any time I heard a tune I could emulate it and play it through pretty well. Sometimes in class I would pretend that I could read music, then listen and put it all together. I was part of a group that won a musical talent show, and that further ignited my passion for music. Playing the drums and guitar was like therapy for me. At those times I was truly engaged.

When I did poorly in the Catholic school I would get a spanking. I did a little better at Highland Park and they moved me ahead. Still, I was sometimes disruptive in class, especially when I thought I was going to be called on. Of course the teacher would ask me to leave the room, but that saved me the embarrassment of admitting I didn't know the correct answer. I would take so long walking down to the principal's office that the class period would be over by the time I got there, and the principal would simply ask, "Where are you supposed to be next?" That solved the problem for the moment, but my anger continued.

In time I learned more about my heritage, American history, and the Civil Rights movement, but I gained this knowledge from the community and not from school. Though my understanding of social justice continued to develop, I was basically done with formal academics by the tenth grade. I had struggled with it, not only academically but also emotionally, and tended to avoid dealing with school-based academic learning at all cost. Eventually, because of my anger, skipping out, and smoking pot, I was kicked out of Highland Park.

At that point, there was no school that would take me other than St. Paul Open School. It was there that I began to develop an understanding of how I could use education to accomplish my goals; that was the beginning of the new me. At St. Paul Open School they explained things to me in a very matter-of-fact way, yet they were so flexible and loose about everything that I was really at a loss as to what was going on.

My mother was as frustrated with me as my former teachers. She was totally fed up and would say that there was nothing she could do for me but put me in the hands of the Lord. All she said she could do was to pray for me! We were all tough, street-smart kids selling weed, smoking pot, and fighting a lot. I never got caught selling drugs, but I did get arrested for assault. I was a dangerous kid carrying both a knife and a gun.

We had gang fights and I got involved in theft, burglary, and even some arson. I was lucky that as a juvenile I didn't wind up doing a lot of time. The judge and probation officers did their best to help me see the destructive nature of my behavior. That didn't all stop when I got to Open School, but over time I settled down and put my life back together. It was their tolerance and willingness to keep nudging me in the right direction that helped get me back on track as a productive citizen. I now realize that I did have one thing that most other kids didn't have— two loving and supportive parents.

David tells his story in an upbeat way. It's almost like he is the parent commenting on the behavior of his child. His candor and self-awareness are refreshing. He is not judgmental about his past, nor is he sure about the origins of his frustration and anger, though it's clear to him that the school system was not turning him on. Certainly his inability to adapt to the standard curriculum left him alone and embarrassed when called upon in class. But I would guess that the underlying reasons for his discomfort at school are more complex. Suffice it to say that there were energy needs inside him that needed an outlet.

What got to me at the Open School was the language they used. They talked about good citizenship and being productive. They talked about problem-solving skills and research skills, and asked me repeatedly how I was going to accomplish my goals. (My goals at the time were to take care of myself and my family.) By asking me those kinds of questions they were able to get through to me. When I would do things to be disruptive or get a rise out the teachers they basically ignored me. It was frustrating at first that I couldn't get attention that way. They would say, "You know, David, the door is not locked. You can leave any time you want to."

At Open School I had to sit down and write up a learning plan. That gave me ownership in the process. I had periodic "adviser" meetings where I would sit with a teacher and discuss what I was doing to accomplish my goals. "This is your plan," they would remind me. "Are you making it work by getting to class and doing your homework?" The next month I would be asked, "Well, David, did you get to your classes on citizenship? How are you coming on the math? Do you need some help on something?" They would go on to say, "David if you didn't complete this community project or finish your homework assignment and aren't taking responsibility for your own behavior, don't expect to be magically successful!"

That's what Patty Breneke told me. She laid that out plain and simple. "We're here to help you, but you have to carry your share of the load," she would say, or "David, do you need to revise your plan? Is what you wrote down still what you want to do?" All of this sounds pretty basic to me today, but for a tenth grader who had never been asked to be part of the process or even think about the future or consider how you get from here to there...it got me thinking differently.

So those kind of things really pulled the rug out from under my rebellious attitude. I was bigger than most of my teachers, but while size mattered on the street, it didn't matter in the classroom. Slowly I learned that no one was going to do it for me. It was so unusual not to have limits and restrictions to fight against. This is when things began to open up for me.

One thing I remember clearly. Every day I would get up and go to school, and in the center of the place there was this big loft. It was made out of carpet and there were these little cubby holes where you could sit down and read a book, take a nap, or talk with someone. I would go in there at 7:30 a.m. and go back to sleep. Joe Nathan, one of the teachers, woke me up and said, "Don't you want to learn how to protect your rights and money?" He was kind of a hippie dude at the time with long hair and casual attire. Of course I said yes, and he replied, "If you're serious come to my class tomorrow afternoon and we'll go over all of that." At the time I had some money from selling pot and I wanted it to be safe.

The class turned out to be really interesting. It was actually like a consumer protection agency. We put the word out around town that if you had been ripped off or taken advantage of, you should let us know and the class would deal with your problem. We acted like an investigative agency, sent letters to the attorney general, and served as a protector for the community.

One of the cases we dealt with was the Hoerner Waldorf Paper Company. A terrible odor would come out of their smokestack every afternoon and stink up the neighborhood. My teachers explained to me that by working on this community project, I could get credits for English, social studies, and even science, because we learned about the scrubbers and other tools for cleaning up the air. All of that seemed interesting to me, and it got me thinking about the rest of the work I needed to do to graduate.

St. Paul Open School was the precursor to the charter school movement, I think, which began in Minnesota before it spread across the country. At that time many teachers and parents were eager to start something new, an education system that emphasized character first and academics second. There were no grades, but you did have to satisfy your credit requirements. It was more of a community-type learning style. The cool thing was that the whole operation was sort of anti-establishment. We had students who were extremely bright, kids who were counter-culture, and then others like me who were angry cut-ups. Learning in this environment was a different kind of experience for me!

The work we did on consumer protection required a lot of dialogue in the classroom, and interestingly enough, that got me into joining the group working in theater. Also, I started doing some traveling with Joe Nathan, talking about the Open School and what was working for me in education.

I'm not good at writing but I do understand what works, and I was able to collaborate with writers who could tell the story of some of the changes we thought should be made in education. That took us to larger cities like Washington, D.C. and New York where Joe had consulting contracts on education reform. We hosted a number of conferences at which I was allowed to express myself, describe my personal experience, and in the process, give my life meaning.

What I found was that this new approach was not only energizing and interesting, but it also involved less hassle and stress than what I had been doing on the street. I was developing new coping skills.

A lot of kids today have no coping skills. Maybe they have only one parent. Some kids don't even have a place to sleep. One of the kids I worked with recently was walking around like an old man. He was embarrassed to tell me that he had been sleeping in a car in sub-zero temperature. He almost lost his toes. Almost one third of the kids we work with today are homeless at some time during the year. Then the Minnesota Department of Education tries to use the same system of measurement for the kids in my school that they use in places like Edina. It's almost insane because you're trying to balance two different worlds. One of the battles I fought with the legislature was when the Minnesota Department of Education tried to label our school as "low achieving." They based that on what is described as an "on time" graduation rate, which they said should be 60 percent. We explained that our kids come to us two years behind in their academics! It doesn't make sense. Why would you identify a school that is trying to fix the problem as being the problem!

The response was always the same: "Well, David, we get federal money to help turn around low-achieving schools like yours." You know that along with the federal money, they come in and tinker with your curriculum. I explained that we're actually a high-performing school when measured against others with the same type of challenged students, such as the Alternative Learning Center or the Contract Alternative.

We don't do this in sports, so why do it with academics? We don't measure the performance of a football player the same way we measure the ability of a gymnast.

These things are so simple that I can't understand how supposedly intelligent leaders can continue to think that way. For the past six years we've been going back and forth with all of that, which drains our energy and diminishes our ability to really help these young people. And that's really sad. With more than two hundred students, our budget exceeds $2 million per year. It's not enough, considering what we're up against, but we could probably make do if we didn't have to spend so much time and money teaching elected officials what they should already know. It's not rocket science, just common sense. In the long run it's a good investment for the state because these people will become productive citizens rather than costing the taxpayers money. The current approach will bankrupt the state in the long run.

But back to my story.

When I graduated from St. Paul Open School I wanted to be a pilot. I went to aviation school and got my commercial license. I loved flying and all the aerodynamics of getting a plane off the ground, the navigation in flight, and getting it back on the ground. It was very humbling because there was no second chance if you screwed up. You just had to get it right. If you pay attention and follow the checklists it's safer than driving a car! I was very proud to get my pilot's license. When I took my father up in the plane and he saw what I had accomplished, he felt that God had answered his prayer.

I did that for a while, and then the music started coming

back into my life. It was the hip-hop era of the mid-1980s. Hip-hop was an expression of the rebellious mood that my generation felt. My friend had a record he wanted me to hear. He said it was the best ever. I asked him if it was better than Herbie Hancock because I was listening to a lot of jazz fusion music at the time. He said yeah! The record was "Rappers Delight," and it just blew me away. After that I listened to a lot of it and then started doing it myself. You see, it's like being a child again, because as you do it you're not afraid of making a mistake. It's almost like babbling, but then you start rhyming it and it comes together. As I explored this new genre I realized that it was a phenomenon on the rise.

I had a relationship with Prince, who grew up in the same community I did. My sister had been in his band, and he spent a lot of time at our house. He had had a hit movie called *Purple Rain* and was getting famous. So I got in touch with him and began to educate him about rap music. At first he was reluctant to get into that and he blew me off for a long time.

I was also friends with some of his band members. They were doing the soundtrack for the first Batman movie—the one with Michael Keaton, Jack Nicholson, and Kim Bassinger. His guitar player, Miko Weaver, showed some of the cuts of the film to me and I wrote a rap to go with the music for that part of the film based on what he was telling me about the story. So I wrote this song, produced it myself, and released it before the movie came out. Warner Brothers somehow got wind of the song and then KMOJ started playing it here in Minnesota. Warner Brother thought that Prince had something to do with it. They called him and he was totally surprised.

Prince then called me up and asked me to come in and do what I called "The Bat Rap."

This is the rap about the bat
that man that is the one in black
like a bat out of hell
he will reveal
screaming down the road
in the Batmobile heading for the crime

only to find nothing but a riddle
you know a rhyme
Jack be nimble Jack be quick

Jack was Jack Nicholson, who played the Joker in the film. So Prince called me out and we started working together on a project. He gave me a record deal and I started working on the soundtrack to his movie.

Prince had a falling out with Warner Brothers. They had all of his master recordings but he wanted to be more on his own, so he changed his name to that symbol. That meant that Warner Brothers could no longer promote him. Finally they released him from the contract, which meant that I was also released. I then opened a recording studio in downtown St. Paul on the skyway level. Kids heard about it and they would sometimes ditch school and come to my studio and hang out. This was the beginning of the High School for Recording Arts.

The kids were hanging around wanting to do hip-hop music while I was trying to serve my clients and make some money. They just wouldn't leave, and finally I let them in the studio and they just blew me away with their creativity. What took me two days to do they could do in thirty minutes! They would actually listen to the music and start writing the raps and then go right into the performance booth and do their thing. I used to get the music from Prince, then work on it in the car and at home, and after a couple of days I would have it down. These kids were amazing.

After they did their rap they started asking me, "How do you copyright?"

They wanted to know everything I knew about the music business. They especially wanted to know how to protect their songs. I told them they had to go to the government document section in the library and get the PA or the SR. I explained that these were the Performing Art or Sound Recording requests, and if they filled them out and sent them to the Library of Congress, they'd get the necessary copyright form. They did get the forms but they couldn't understand the questions. So I asked them, "How come you guys aren't in school?" Their response was, "Fuck school ... we don't want to go there!" All of that reminded me of my own history.

Still, I was struck by the genius of these kids, and I told them that if they could do this stuff they could also get through high school, because I didn't start doing this stuff until I was thirty years old.

Then one day I read in the paper that Dr. Wayne Jennings, my old high school principal, was opening a charter school. He had created what was called the Community Learning Model. I called him up and told him about these ten kids that were coming up to my studio every day and bugging the heck out of me. He came over and visited that very same day.

Dr. Jennings said he would enroll these ten kids in his charter school, but that they would come to my studio each day instead of his school. Our curriculum was based on the day's newspaper. We made the kids chronicle three articles on national and international news from the local papers and three articles on state and local news. Then they had to comment on what they'd just read, and after that they could go into the studio and put it all in rap format. This gave them credits for current events, social studies, writing, and so forth, and it gave us a crude indication of their skill levels. Teachers from Dr. Jennings' school would then come over in the afternoon and follow up on the core skills with the kids.

Within two months there were fifty kids on the waiting list to enroll in the pilot project, entirely due to word-of-mouth advertising. This was in 1997. By 2005 two hundred kids were enrolled. Any kid who wanted to do a rap would get in the studio, and we'd give them a tape that they could play for their friends. Of course their friends would ask, "Where is this studio at?"

As the program became more popular, Dr. Jennings urged me to apply for an independent charter school status. He's in his eighties now, still sharp as a tack, and serving on our board. Because of him, I feel that I've become an expert at dealing with "at risk" kids, and this is now my life's work. We're in a new building now at 1166 University Avenue, which is right on the new light rail line, and this will allow us to expand to two hundred and fifty students.

So, as I said, this has become my life's work. Some of the work these kids have done is amazing. They have done projects for Verizon Wireless, Exxon Mobile, and State Farm Insurance. They do the music, the video, and all the content. This has helped our fund-raising efforts. State Farm Insurance and Lube Tech have been major funders, above and beyond what the state provides for charter schools.

In terms of statewide policies that impact education, I think Minnesota has to take time out to think about whether our current policies are helping kids who have dropped out of the system or been kicked out for disciplinary reasons. The current main line system just doesn't work for every kid, so we have to reshape education policies and programs to fit where they're at. We have to be tolerant and patient, and realize that for some students, learning just doesn't happen overnight. If we can have the flexibility to work with these kids and relate better to what turns them on, I think we can work miracles.

While we want to prepare kids for college, we also need to recognize that every kid doesn't need to go to college. Who says you can't be a successful metal worker or carpenter or chef? Many of these kids simply don't have the means to finance a college education, and in any case, you have to remember that for quite a few, the main issue for many years was simply to survive and cope in a hostile or broken social and family environment. Our kids don't all wind up as musicians. They learn about production, engineering, electronics, graphic design, photography, the law, and the business of music. They may start out thinking they're going to become a rap star like the ones they see on TV, but our school exposes them to a variety of different disciplines. For example, twice a year I have the kids tear apart the studio and clean it up, applying new technology where needed. They're plugging this thing into that, and figuring out about polarity and other such things. It opens up a whole new world for them and prepares them to become electricians. So for many, the interest in rap and music leads on to other areas of learning and growth.

David looks younger than his fifty-five years. He tells his story slowly and with passion for these kids, who obviously remind him of his own challenging teenage years. While his frustration with statewide policies, which still lack adequate support for kids with unusual learning styles, is obvious, he remains optimistic about the future.

The results of his work are gaining recognition from elected officials, and his support from businesses continues to grow. Projections for the traditional white workforce show little to no growth over the next few decades, so future workforce needs will have to be met by the expanding communities of color. Thus the long-term demographics favor more support for effective alternative-education schools. But because schools chase the dollars, and measurement standards for performance are stacked against alternative schools, we continue to underinvest in them, even though they advance our long-term interest.

We all read the school ratings published each year. The system continues to rate the schools based on a yardstick that is the same regardless of the economic, racial, and ethnic background of the kids. While no one should advocate lowering the performance standard bar, we should do what we do with beginning athletes and set the bar at appropriate levels given the varying skill levels of the students. It's the issue of relative performance versus absolute performance. Dave Ellis has figured this out and hopefully his message will create change for the better in the future.

Who helped Dave Ellis break out of his destructive teenage lifestyle? There were a few teachers who bucked the system and tried to accommodate his tactile learning style in public school. But it was the open school and the wisdom of teachers like Joe Nathan that began to speak a language he could relate to. The Open School specialized in the type of education that, instead of being focused on what the teachers know about their subject, starts with an assessment of what will "turn on" this particular child. As they told Dave, "The door is not locked ... you can leave any time you want!"

Bibi Abdalla

"When we left home, we were dressed in our traditional Somali coverings, but when we got to school we took off the outer covering and converted to American style so we would fit in. We naturally converted back on the way home since our parents would be furious if they found out."

My interview with Bibi took place in my home in northeast Minneapolis, not far from where she has an apartment. Her maturity and breadth of experience are well beyond what one might expect from a twenty-five-year-old native of Somalia. Her voice is calm and her English perfect. She speaks slowly, and one knows that there is deep conviction in her observations about her life experiences in America. She loves this country and is not shy about wanting to make it better.

I came here when I was eight years old. The war started in 1989, the year I was born up north in Somalia. I was about one year old when we left Somalia and went to Kenya. There we spent eight years in refugee camps, moving from one place to another. My older siblings did not want to wait for permission to come to America. The waiting list was very long. One went to

Australia, another to Italy, and eventually we just got spread all over the world. My mother and my younger siblings and I ended up in Minnesota. Our story here in the states began in Minneapolis, where I started in the third grade. We lived in southeast Minneapolis near Clinton and Franklin Avenues. One day in the late 1990s I got off the bus, and someone got shot! That was when the city was called Murderapolis. My mother decided to move since we had come here to get away from violence. I have nine siblings, and we were living in subsidized rental housing. We moved to Skyline Towers in St. Paul, which was subsidized rental housing managed by Common Bond Communities. That was when I was eleven.

There were many Somalis living in Skyline Towers. This was a tall apartment building near the freeway that had been redeveloped for low-income housing by Common Bond. In the beginning there wasn't much to do. Every parent was new to the country and frightened because they didn't know who to trust. We children were not allowed to go out, especially the girls. The boys had more freedom. The first few years it was home and then to school and then back home again. Then a woman named Debra Lande started the teen program. This was mostly for girls in middle school and those starting high school. There is a huge difference between how we children viewed our new culture and the traditional approach taken by our parents. We kids were trying to balance these two cultures, and there were many things we could not discuss with our parents. You see, when you go to school you are expected to be a certain person and when you are at home you are supposed to be another person. My father is now ninety years old. Before the war in Somalia he taught, was in business, and also spent time in the military. Fortunately my parents are both healthy.

When we left home each morning we were dressed in our traditional Somali coverings, but when we got to school we took off the outer covering and converted to American style so we would fit in. We naturally converted back on the way home since our parents would be furious if they found out. So here we were as kids growing up, when the hormones are kicking in and there is so much physical and emotional change going on, and you can't even talk to your parents about it. There were drugs and sex—a lot of crazy things were going on. Even the words "drugs" and "cigarettes" were taboo in our culture. At that time if we used those words we would probably have been kicked out of the house for a while. Today this has changed somewhat. At that time there was a lot of mistrust between parents and kids. My parents didn't speak much English so they couldn't be sure we were telling them the truth about what went on in school and what our teachers thought about our performance.

There were some kids from troubled neighborhoods in Minneapolis that were getting into gangs and drugs and stuff like that, and it was very frightening to us. Some of those people tried to influence us. What Debra Lande's teen program did was to give my friends and me a place where we could discuss things like drugs, sex, money, cultural differences, our education, and how to get along better with our parents. The program became, in a way, another kind of family for us. Debra and other staff members encouraged us to believe in the future—that things would change for the better, and that we would have fulfilling lives if we just did our very best each day. Mothers were OK with the program, first because it was only for the girls, and second because it was set it up like it was a job. We received a small stipend each week if we came so we had some spending money. It's important, when you're trying to fit into a new culture, to be able to buy some of the simple little things that the new culture expects. The older kids tutored the younger ones, and the mothers looked at it as if it were job at MacDonald's, rather than simple charity. This program was such a great help to all of us.

The next step for me was to take advantage of Common Bond's Advantage Center. The pressure from my parents early on made me fully aware that I was expected to go to school. Fine, but why? I was seeing kids who worked at MacDonald's making good money, so what was the point of going to school? That extra money helped the families a lot and gave the kids a sense of accomplishment. The downside of all of that, of course, was that it took their attention away from school. The people at the Advantage Center helped me work through all that. They helped me prioritize my goals and were there to help with homework, language, and the cultural adjustments. Instead of making a lot of money at Target or places like that, I could work two hours at the Advantage Center's computer lab and make enough to get by. So while my education came first, my basic needs were also being met, and the Advantage Center became like a second mother to me. I believe this service helped the girls much more than the boys, unfortunately.

One of the boys in Skyline Towers got a nearly perfect score on his SATs. He always talked about the future and what he wanted to make of his life. Sadly, the influence from some of the gangs got to him. In his high school junior year, gang members approached him and introduced him to some young girls who were into sex and alcohol and then later drugs. He got involved with them, and then the gang members told him that he had to pay for the fun he was having by going to work for them. That was the end for him and he wound up in prison. This was a kid who could have gotten into Harvard if he wanted to. The process is carefully executed by the gang, and for a kid who wants to be accepted, the temptation can be strong.

The most important thing for me was staying focused and then knowing where to go for help, and the Advantage Center made that work. Volunteers from various colleges came in and tutored us. This not only helped us improve our grades, but it showed us that there was a world out there beyond the confines of our apartment building. We felt quite confined at times, and to have an ethnically and racially diverse group of college-age volunteers coming in gave us a better glimpse of the wider world. I went from a D to a B in physics because a physicist was willing to work with me—until 3:00 a.m. some days. He mentored me, and I could tell that he knew what it was to work hard. We would go to lunch and visit his home, and he was like a father to me. He worked with me for four years, until my junior year in college. This was another important resource that Common Bond's Advantage Center made available to me.

Another organization that Common Bond referred me to was Admission Possible, now called College Possible. In my sophomore year in high school a young woman named Khuluni, just three years older than me, introduced me to the program. She and other volunteers helped me learn what was required to go to college. They worked with me on my SAT preparation, helped me find the right college, and then showed me how to get a scholarship. Khulani was Somali and Oramu, and it was natural for us to help one another. The older girls like Khulani could tell which students wanted to improve their lives and which simply wanted to enjoy the pleasure of the moment. Many of this latter group married early and are still in the welfare system.

My first inclination was to go college someplace far away—a place that was warm. Many other kids my age had the same dream. Then my father reminded me that to graduate from college with mountains of debt would limit both me and my family; it was not a good idea. He also was opposed on cultural grounds to paying interest on debt. I took his advice and went to the place that gave me the biggest scholarship.

My choice was the College of Saint Benedict. It turned out to be an excellent choice. It was 2005 and I was the only Somali student; there were few minorities from any part of the world. I had no friends other than the Somali kids I'd grown up with, so I felt very much alone that first year.

My academic program was called the Intercultural Leadership, Education and Development Fellowship Program. The students in this program were all from low-income families of Asian, African, or African American heritage. Thanks to College Possible I was able to learn that college was possible and then the steps needed to make it happen.

There is another challenge—the difficulty of staying in college once you get there. For foreign students like me there is the ongoing issue of whether to spend $200 on textbooks or to send that money back home to your native country where you know life is very hard. That was not my problem because my family lived here in Minnesota, but still the financial pressures were great. Many of the relatives of immigrant families with kids in college think that they must be rich so their expectations for interest-free loans and financial support are high. The staff at Admission Possible was there to offer support whenever I needed it.

Eventually I learned how to get out of my bubble and start to take risks meeting other kids. It was my older sister who shook me up. She said, "Bibi, you are the one who has to figure out how to relate to these Minnesotans." She advised me to think about what they were interested in and then develop the relationship from that point forward. So I did, and that helped a lot. So just as Common Bond built the ladder that allowed me to go to college, Admission Possible and Saint Benedict's taught me about this new world I was living in. I was no longer just a Somali but had been transformed into a Somali American.

Near the end of college, while at a retreat at Harvard, I was introduced to a program called CORO—a public leadership development program. I flew to St. Louis and applied, was accepted, and then worked for the program for one year at their regional office there in Missouri. The program teaches you how to be a leader, regardless of the specific environment—government, business, or non-profit. It's a holistic approach to understanding how these sectors work together to create the society we have today.

When I returned to the Twin Cities I reconnected with a trustee of Saint Benedict's called Sherry who mentored me with respect to job opportunities. She told me a lot about Cargill, and so I applied there and was accepted in their basic business managers training program. There were few minorities at Cargill at that time, so this transition was difficult. However, I had a really great mentor there who helped me better understand the culture of the organization. My own style of using a gentle approach to interpersonal relationships differed considerably from the traditionally more direct and time-focused approach common in business. After training I was sent to Iowa City, Iowa. Cargill makes sure executive trainees experience life in the regions where the grain is grown, which makes sense. There I learned about the science of making animal feed. Being the only person of color involved in the operation, I found living there extremely lonely and frightening. I just didn't feel comfortable living in a small town like that. When my father became sick I requested to be transferred back to the Twin Cities.

Cargill has been flexible, allowing me to work from home when I need to, so I can be there for my parents. However, there is this thing called perception, and I worry that some of my colleagues think I'm not getting my work done. I believe that what matters is that we do our work well, to create value for others. This, in addition to getting a paycheck, can be very rewarding. Sometimes in corporate America I think this satisfaction gets lost when managers think there is only one way to get things done.

Everyone needs to feel that they're part of building something important. If you want to truly feel like you're contributing, you need to be encouraged to take risks and suggest new approaches. Some managers, I believe, focus so much on not upsetting the status quo that they become reactive and lose their focus on the future. They become risk averse. If I don't feel that I'm contributing, I can take my skills somewhere else. I know I'm rambling a bit, but I feel sad for those who feel trapped in their work. My point is that I can be just as productive working at home as in an office cubicle, yet some managers don't believe that and expect you to be sitting at your desk every day.

Many of the things we have created in business have come out of research that was done some time ago. I think American business has to instill more creativity in its workers to counterbalance the assembly line approach that's cost effective in the short run but may miss out on glowing opportunities in the long run.

The U.S. is currently home to 45 million foreign-born people. That's 20 percent of the world total, and four times more than Russia, who is number two on the list. Nevertheless, I believe that the United States would do even better economically if it accepted more immigrants each year. Most refugees, when given the kind of support I was given, are hard workers who are willing to try new ways to solve old problems.

Remember that we have struggled and taken risks every step of the way to get here. We have had to relate to the culture of our parents while at the same time trying to fit into this new and unfamiliar world. We have learned a new language and struggled to master the nuances involved in communicating with key groups in business, government, and non-profits. We have adopted the United States as our new home. We know we cannot go back to our native lands. We have the advantage of truly recognizing the greatness of this country, while also recognizing that it would be possible to make it work even better. At age twenty-five I feel confident that I can be a creative citizen. I am not afraid to speak out, and I look forward to the future with confidence. So many have helped me along the way, and I am not about to let them down.

One can speculate about how Bibi's life would have developed without help from Common Bond, College Possible, the University of Saint Benedict, and good mentorship at Cargill. She believes that she and her family would have required public assistance for an extended period of time. Without Common Bond and support from their Advantage Center, the other links in this stepping-stone success story would probably never have been forged. As she reflects on what might make America work better, I was reminded of DeToqueville's ability to see certain things in American culture and economic processes that Americans themselves were not aware of at the time. Once again I was reminded that other than our native population we are all refugees or immigrants of one kind or another. This has been the greatness of America, and as long as new immigrants remain welcome, I believe we can look to the future with confidence.

Kandy McDonal

"Kids shouldn't get the short end of the stick just because their mother can't find work. These kids are our future. We have to develop early on their love of learning so they don't wind up on the street and get into trouble."

Kandy McDonal and her two children live in the Midway area of St. Paul, Minnesota. Her work has allowed her to rent a modest two-bedroom home, a first for this family. There is a sense of stability to this home, with evidence that the two kids are well supplied with the things kids need to learn and recreate. This home represents another successful step in the long and difficult journey Kandy has made from her early years growing up in poverty with highly dysfunctional parents in Peoria, Illinois.

I have two kids, Kendrick and Mariah, ages eight and four. I moved to the Midway area of St. Paul in 2007. I was going up to the Syndicate Building in St. Paul one day to arrange for some assistance with my heating bill, and I saw a sign that said Head Start. So I enrolled my son, Kendrick, in the program, and that's where it all began. At the time I was receiving assistance from the county for child care for my son. I was working now and then through a temporary employment service; they set me up with a stint at Wells Fargo, for example. Somewhere along the line, when Kendrick's child care support was ending, I heard about a scholarship program through an organization called Think Small. This would take care of Kendrick until he was in kindergarten. He was two and a half at the time. The scholarship meant that I didn't have to worry about the co-pay the county required or the paperwork involved. County support would have required submitting forms showing how many hours a week I worked and how much money I made per hour because Kendrick's day care financial support was based on those figures. When you're a single parent, remembering to file all that paperwork can be hard. So I was thrilled that he could go every day for eight hours—forty hours a week! It was a relief to me that I no longer had to worry about whether I was making enough for him to go for a full day. It didn't matter whether I was working or not. And it helped him become better prepared for kindergarten!

There is energy in the way Kandy McDonal expresses herself that for me represents the essence of the American Dream. There is little evidence of bitterness or embarrassment regarding the troubled family she grew up with.

My upbringing was a lot different from what I'm providing my kids today. I'm not ashamed of what I went through. My dad was a drug dealer, and my mom was never there for us. She was smoking crack. I am the only girl in a family with five boys. I'm the oldest and had to care for the others. I hope my kids never wind up on the streets and experience some of the things I had to live with. My mom is doing OK now and lives six blocks away. She was put away for six years, which meant she missed a big chunk of our lives. When I was seven, both my parents were gone. I wound up cooking and doing the wash and all the rest. My dad would send money, but he couldn't be there for us.

I grew up pretty fast. When I was a high school senior in Peoria my dad was still on the run. The four youngest boys were shielded from the trouble. When my mom went to jail, her dad and uncle came and got the boys and brought them to St. Paul. I was able to stay in Peoria until I graduated. Then in 2001 I came to Minnesota and got my degree as a paralegal at the Minnesota College of Business. I graduated in 2005 and walked across the platform pregnant with my first child.

For the past ten years I have held a variety of customer service jobs with companies like Wells Fargo and US Bank, so I've developed a wide range of skills. One of my jobs was to open the Old Navy store at the Brookdale Mall. Currently I work for Creative Care Resources, serving vulnerable adults who are autistic. I prepare their meals, help them dress, and work with them on their sensory routines. These are adults with a mental age of between five and seven. They couldn't function in mainstream autism facilities so several of the clinic owners set up this special facility for them. I enjoy the work as it draws on all the skills I've learned. The frustration level of the clients can get very high at times. What I do is teach them how to keep themselves calm and remind them that they're safe. I work thirty-six hours a week at $13 per hour. Most of that work is during twelve-hour shifts on weekends, so I can be home with the kids much of the week. This means that I can help the kids with their homework and still have time to prepare meals and be there for them. The fathers pick the kids up for the weekend and that frees me up to work.

Kandy is confident and joyful as she sings the praises of the day care assistance she received for Kendrick and Mariah. Her story is as good a testimonial as one could find on the relationship between affordable day care and the ability to find a living-wage job.

When my daughter, Mariah, was six weeks old, I started sending her to the same day care where Kendrick was going. Once again the support I received for day care was based on how many hours I worked. When you go off the Minnesota day care subsidy called MFIP [Minnesota Family Investment Plan] you have one year to prepare yourself to be on your own in terms of paying for day care. MFIP was not that helpful for me because it gave cash assistance of only $437 a month and didn't look at your basic costs. Since Kendrick's father paid nearly $400 a month in child support, I was just about able to make up the difference. I have also been on a plan called Stand Alone Food and Health Care, which doesn't pay cash but does look at what you pay out in a month, and that program actually helps you. I still have a scale that I cannot exceed, but I get my food support and health care, in addition to making $13 per hour at work. That income, plus child support from the boy's father and the day care scholarship, helps us get by each month. Where I live now I pay $995 a month in rent plus heat, electrical, and all the rest. Think Smart now pays Mariah's day care scholarship. As you know, quality day care can cost as much as $900 or more a month. So the scholarships make a huge difference and allow me to work forty hours a week!

At $13 an hour, Kandy is earning about $24,000 per year, before adding on her child support payments of

approximately $4,800 and food stamps valued at about $5,000 per year. Her rental payments would take about 36 percent of her gross income. Quality day care for both children would consume all of the rest of her income, leaving nothing for food, clothing, transportation, or utilities. In her case, quality day care assistance opens the way to a full-time job. It also reduces the odds of the two children eventually winding up as dependent on public assistance of some kind. Child support continues until the children are eighteen.

Kendrick is now eight and doing great in school. When he had the day care scholarship at the quality place they would bring books out to the house and show us how to work with him on his reading and other early learning requirements. Mariah's program is a full eight-hour day. The line between success and failure is a very thin one for people like us. If I hadn't been able to find my current job at the group home, Mariah would probably have only two hours of day care a day. That's how the formula works. Then she would be home for the rest of the day and I would have to be there and wouldn't be able to work full time. Affordable high quality day care is absolutely critical so the parent can work and the child can learn! I can work until 4:30 p.m. and then pick her up. It's perfect. Earlier this year, when I was unemployed, her day care funding was about to dry up.

That same night at Mariah's school, they had Family Fun Night and announced that scholarships were available. I mean it was a miracle that we got that scholarship from Think Small because it took a while for me to find another job. That's how scary this life can be when you have a modest income and children that you want to raise well. The scholarships are quite limited and restricted to a certain geographic area. It's a hard support system to navigate for those of us who want to work. People like me who live in the Midway area have to go to downtown St. Paul to get all the paperwork done. I'm lucky because I have my old Ford Explorer.

It makes no sense to me that we have to pay to send our kids to pre-kindergarten. This is where the learning process starts. Why do you have to wait for the kids to enter kindergarten for the education to be paid for? That just baffles me! The way the system is working now is just a bunch of crap! Pardon my words, but the kids shouldn't get the short end of the stick just because their mother can't find work. These kids are our future.

We have to develop early on their love of learning so they don't wind up on the street and get into trouble. Of course the teachers have to be paid, and they should be if they pass the requirements. Minnesota taxpayers will be better off if they make sure these kids are taught and taught well.

Right now I'm on strict "Stand Alone" in terms of benefits. This means that I don't have to depend upon MFIP, which has a five-year time limit on cash assistance. I can keep MFIP as a last resort if everything else fails. For example, under MFIP I can get emergency assistance if I lose my job. I had to resort to that in the past or we would have been put out on the street. The five-year limit on cash assistance is cumulative, so I need to keep that as a last resort.

"Stand Alone" means I get food stamps and medical assistance for me and the kids. Food stamps were worth $537 per month for a family of three, but Congress recently reduced it to less than $500 per month. That almost gets me through the month. The medical assistance coverage is good and includes prescriptions so the kids are fully covered. For me there is a small co-pay at Walgreens or CVS. The kids can go into day care six weeks after they're born. When I was working and making about $12 per hour, I used to pay $700 per month for day care for both children. I don't have family or friends who could care for my children, so I had to find a licensed day care provider. Infants are more expensive than toddlers because you pay for formula and other stuff little kids need. That's about $8,400 a year out of my gross pay before taxes of about $24,000. That's a lot when you have to figure in rent, gas, maintenance on the car, clothes, and everything else. We were going to three separate locations every morning.

Time and scheduling is another constraint since the kids have to be dropped off at day care before work and picked up after work.

It gets easier once they're off to kindergarten. Day care assistance is the only way you can find the time to look for a job when you have young children. The kids want to go to school and learn. Without day care the questions keep coming up, "Mom, why can't I go to school today?" They love the field trips and associating with teachers and other kids. The scholarship program allows Mariah to stay in her area and not get distracted by my job search and the frustrations that go with that. This program has allowed my kids to learn and be safe. We live very frugally on a tight budget and don't go out much.

The Think Small scholarship means that my daughter comes home with books and some homework and is excited about learning. Mariah, at age four, can write her first and last name, and she can count from one to forty. She knows her ABCs and is doing great. At the school they have the kids sing and dance so it's a well-rounded program. These kids absorb everything at that age, and without this kind of top-quality program, kindergarten would be rough for them. Kids I know who haven't had quality pre-K don't have the same love for learning my kids have. It's sad because those kids lag behind the pre-K children both socially and academically. I've done it and so have my siblings, so there is really no excuse why others can't succeed!

I asked Kandy if she thought our welfare support system encouraged some people to game the system and avoid seeking work. She admitted that some people from poor family backgrounds might be inclined to do that. However, she also stated that at some point you have to grow up and make your own choices, and the welfare support system helps those who are willing to help themselves. She admits it's not perfect but she strongly believes that if you want to make it, you can. Kandy can't think of any particular mentor that inspired her to work hard in school and succeed. She believes that her family situation caused her to grow up fast and that meant taking responsibility for herself and her siblings at an early age. Kandy says she had a solid understanding of what she didn't want to be, and that caused her to put together her life plans at an early age.

Pa Kong Lee

"I don't think I would have made it to college without College Possible. While I can't be sure, I think that the cultural pressure from home and the lack of intensive academic and moral support from overworked high school counselors might well have put me on a different track."

The roots of this story go back to the Vietnam War. It brings a young child born in a refugee camp in southeast Asia to the Twin Cities, where her life is changed dramatically because of a remarkable program created by Jim McCorkell, a young social entrepreneur and graduate of Carlton College in Northfield, Minnesota.

My name is Pa Kong Lee. You can call me Pa. I was born on June 15, 1986, in a refugee camp called Ban Vinai in Thailand. I came to the United States with my mom and two siblings on March 12, 1992. We came because of the aftermath of the Vietnam War. During the war the Hmong were helping the Americans as guerrilla fighters. It was referred to as "the Secret War." After the fall of Saigon in 1975, the Hmong were scattered everywhere. Some were able to come to America because of their assistance to the Americans during the war.

Some were left behind, while others were resettled in other countries.

My parents were originally from Laos, and my dad was involved in the Vietnam conflict at an early age. He met my mom in Laos and took her with him to Thailand. After the war my aunt, who was already living in Massachusetts, sponsored my mom, my siblings, and me to come to the United States. We lived in Massachusetts for a short time before joining my dad in Minneapolis in 1993. We lived in south Minneapolis, where I started school in the first grade. Later we moved to the north Minneapolis neighborhood where I largely grew up and now live. After high school, I attended college at Hamline University, where I persued my undergraduate degree, in St. Paul.

I grew up in a traditional Hmong family, which was somewhat patriarchal. In my family, my role as a Hmong female was to go to school, maintain good grades, return home, and make sure my siblings did their homework. I was also responsible for helping my mom making meals and keeping the house clean.

As a result, in high school I was not able to play sports or participate in other extracurricular activities. I first attended Bethune Elementary School, Olson Middle School, and finally Patrick Henry High School. There was a lot of diversity and several other Hmong students in the schools that I attended.

All in all it was a happy experience. As the eldest child, I was responsible for a lot. My mom spoke no English, so I was the interpreter even during school conferences with my teachers! We also lived in public housing, and I grew up living on welfare. I assisted in completing all the paperwork for the various programs. I sometimes felt ashamed that my family was dependent on public support. I knew my parents wanted to break out of that system and recognized that if this was to happen, we children would be the ones to do it. I also knew that education was the key.

The area in north Minneapolis that I grew up in was called "the projects." In recent years new homes and apartments have been put up and it's called Heritage Park. Many Hmong families actually liked the density of the projects because the extended family members lived close to one another. We became scattered after the new development was completed. It's nice living by people who look like you and talk the same language when you first go to a new country. When we moved to the Harrison neighborhood, we were one of the first Asian families to live in a predominantly black area, and that was scary for my mom, especially when we kids were gone all day at school. Our home was broken into a few times, and while at school I would worry about my mom.

My teachers at Patrick Henry were very good. There, I had a pretty diverse group of friends who were very supportive. English was my favorite subject, and my teachers were terrific.

At that time, it was not the usual thing for girls my age to think about college. In many families, the expectation was that you would help your family until you got married and start to raise a family yourself. My parents, however, encouraged me to get a job. It was my sophomore year at Patrick Henry when I first heard about Admission Possible [now known as College Possible] and decided to sign up. The program was designed to help students like me go to college. You do the testing in the junior year and become deeply involved in the senior year. While I knew that I wanted to go to college, I also knew that I had to find a school away from where my parents lived because as the oldest, I would still be expected to help at home with the other kids if I was nearby.

So I signed up with College Possible. I never thought I would get accepted because I knew nothing about college. Meeting the second site coordinator, Willy Tully, and being assigned to a coach, Erika Huss, who had been a Peace Corps volunteer after college and was working on her masters degree, was inspiring. Together they convinced me that I was qualified to go beyond a community or technical college. When I spoke to my mom about this she was worried and said that we couldn't afford it. She was concerned about the long-term burden of college debt and was troubled by the thought that I would be leaving my role as a Hmong female behind. This was all a struggle for me, too, having to be a different person at home than at school.

My coach kept me on track preparing for ACTs, learning how to apply for college and then how to request financial aid. It really opened my eyes to find there were so many scholarship opportunities out there. In the end, I applied for twenty-two scholarships and was successful with four! I was encouraged that there were so many people who wanted to help. My first choice was Hamline University. Though attending there did require some student loans, I felt the private university experience Hamline offered was worth the expense.

I graduated. After college, I went to work with AmeriCorps as a Volunteer in Service to America (VISTA) serving as a volunteer coordinator for Phalen Lake Hmong Studies magnet school in St. Paul under the host organization Minnesota Literacy Council. I would go into the community, build partnership with community colleges, universities, and colleges, and recruit students to join our literacy tutoring program and work as tutors in the classroom.

As my VISTA experience was ending, I applied to the US Peace Corps (PC). Working with a huge number of refugee and immigrants at the school, I felt it was the right time to do something different and hoped that the experience would help me see what I want to do in the future. Because of my medical history with epilepsy, it took me a year to complete all the paperwork and find a country that could offer the medical support that I needed. Finally, after completing everything, I was invited to go to the Philippines as a youth development worker in May 2010.

In August 2010 I went to the Philippines. For two years I worked with a faith-based organization called Kapatiran-Kaunlaran Foundation, Inc. (KKFI). There I worked with one of their service programs called Gilead Center. Gilead Center is a temporary shelter for street kids, abandoned and neglected, poor children. I worked with a counterpart—a host national—teaching the kids crafts and basic life and leadership skills and introducing them to empowerment opportunities. I also co-facilitated HIV/AIDS training with other PC volunteers in my region. While serving in the Philippines, I was exposed to TB and dengue fever and recovered from both. After my service overseas, I traveled for a bit before coming home in December 2012.

In January, I tutored at a Hmong charter school in St. Paul called Community School of Excellence. I have recently been accepted for graduate school at Brandeis University in Waltham, Massachusetts, and will start this fall. I plan to study Sustainable International Development. Due to my involvement in the Peace Corps and AmeriCorps, the school was able to offer me a good financial aid package.

When I asked Pa Kong about her grades, which had been first rate, she just laughed and said, "They have been pretty OK." Her modesty was evident and her style so relaxed that

it fully masked the struggles she had endured along the way. She continued to praise Erika, her coach at College Possible, who she said was always there for her, reminding her to prepare each week and even including a car ride to take the ACT exams if she didn't have transportation. She commented that sometimes it's important to have someone to share her struggles with. Erika met with her parents, which assured them that Pa Kong was working hard. She says that it's critical that parents trust this system because it's promoting something foreign to them—a college education. Her sister, Mai-Eng, has followed in her footsteps by joining College Possible, graduating from the University of St. Thomas, and completing her masters in social work from the University of Wisconsin–Madison. Her brother Fue recently graduated from Carleton College in Northfield, Minnesota.

Pa Kong believes that College Possible is important because it fills a void at area schools. She feels that the regular school counselors are so overburdened that they simply don't know the students well and often cannot relate to the cultural differences involved in dealing with them. Pa Kong felt comfortable with her coach, who knew her name, set time aside for her, and offered advice when she most needed it. The fact that her coach knew her so well also helped her suggest the colleges best suited for Pa both academically and financially.

I don't think I would have made it to college without College Possible. While I can't be sure, I think that the cultural pressure from home and the lack of intensive academic and moral support from overworked high school counselors might well have put me on a different track. Erika helped me set goals and understand that there was great long-term benefit in a college education. So it has become a struggle between whether I should help my mom now or later with a college education. This was not an easy choice to make but I believe I made the correct decision. When I finish graduate school, I want to focus on gender and youth development. I grew up in a patriarchal society, so gender equality is important to me. I believe that our future is in the hands of today's youth. I don't know if it's possible, but some day I want to work for UNICEF, helping them design and implement programs for women and children.

John Turnipseed

"With eighty gang members I ran that prison for three and a half years. We controlled prostitution, drugs, living arrangements, how they did their time, phone calls, and we bought and sold anything anybody wanted. I kept power by supplying the five guys that worked for me. They were all in for murder."

When I met with John Turnipseed at his office at Urban Ventures Leadership Foundation in south Minneapolis, his presence and professionalism matched that of business executives I had met with during my nearly forty-year career in financial services. There was no evidence that sitting before me was a middle-aged African American man who had been part of one of the region's more active crime families. There was a spiritual quality to his demeanor. As he told his tale of destructive behavior, I felt like he could be describing someone else's life—not his own.

While this is a story about one man who was both a born leader and a highly skilled criminal, it's also a story about another man who never stopped believing in John's redemptive qualities. In addition, it's a story about a legal system that sometimes can spot when the timing is right for a convicted felon to turn his life around.

I was born in 1954, the first child of a Southern Baptist Christian family, in Selma, Alabama. My earliest childhood memories are of helping to pick cotton, being very involved with my family in church, raising chickens in the back yard, and holding choir practice at our home. There was plenty of food so I was never hungry. Nobody cussed or drank. I never had a spanking. My mother and father were very nice to me. Grandmothers lived on either side of us. One was very nice and the other a little cranky, but we all got along well. There were grandfathers but I don't remember ever seeing them. We moved to Minnesota when I was eight and lived within a block of where we are now at 31st Street and First Avenue.

It was after our move that I remember being hungry for the first time. My father had moved here before us, and I soon learned that he had a girlfriend who was not my mom. My dad was drinking then and had become violent. I would ride with him in his car and he would go to this other woman's house. I later knew her as my stepmother. My father was an angry drunk, and when he drank he would start hitting my mom. That was my introduction to violence.

My mother worked, and my father was hardly ever home except to beat her. I spent most of my days and nights worrying about him coming home. I would hide stuff like knives and belts so he wouldn't use them on my mother. I had five little brothers who I fed and took care of. Going to school was quite an adventure because I couldn't tell anyone what was going on at home. The beatings my mom received were very violent, and the only way I could stop my dad was to jump in my mom's lap and try to hang on to her as my dad tried to pull me away.

At school they thought that I was a problem child. School work at Horace Mann was easy and my homework was a breeze.

They even put me on medication because I would become agitated and start fighting. The reason I fought was to get them to send me home so I could be there with my mother in the event my dad came home early. I was angry at school and was bullied because I was this kid, Turnipseed, with a funny last name, who was skinny and had this southern drawl that people thought was funny. That's what I remember about my early school life. School was not very productive for me.

At home I would read to my brothers and help them with their school work. I was essentially home schooled though my mother didn't have more than a sixth-grade education. She was very smart and wanted us to be very smart.

I found relief in sports. I played basketball and football in Powderhorn Park for coach Andy Drinkwile. My parents never came to any of my games, so the coach kind of took me under his wing. That was my only real form of relief as a kid. By the time I was twelve I was influenced by a cousin of mine from Chicago named Tommy. He was a big guy—even bigger than my dad, who was six-one. He made my dad leave my mother alone, and he taught me to be violent, too. He would make me fight, gave me my first gun, and set up my first sexual experience with an older woman—a prostitute he knew who lived in our neighborhood.

By the time I was sixteen I had been into everything, including armed robbery. I had started drinking at twelve and taking stuff like red devils and a type of speed called white cross. People would make it like they make meth today. I would be high every day and started skipping school. It was at that time that I started talking to my brothers about killing my dad. In short, I was a juvenile delinquent. My mother couldn't handle me, and at age seventeen I pulled a gun on my father and told him that if he ever hit my mother again I'd kill him. That was the last time he hit my mother. He knew I was serious because while we never spoke much it was the first time I had ever used that tone of voice with him. I was glad he backed off because I would have killed him and wound up in jail. I had already been in the juvenile justice system's county home school for boys at Glen Lake with a group of very violent young men like myself. We all had guns.

A year earlier, at age sixteen, I had been introduced to gangs. Mind you, I had grown up in a Christian family, went to church regularly, and was going to be a preacher. Where I grew up in Alabama that was the highest distinction you could achieve. Preachers were more important than the president. Everybody loved and listened to them. I would practice and imitate the preacher after the service. I loved church, and my dad had been a deacon. Our church was Southern Baptist Pentecostal and we went every Sunday. When we came to Minnesota we stopped going to church. My mother was bruised from being beat up, and I turned away from a God that would allow kids to go hungry and mothers to get beat up. I dedicated my life to making money any way I could. I first started stealing to feed my family. My mother would work from mid-afternoon until late at night, but that was not enough money to house and feed our large family. The welfare support would run out real quick. My dad never contributed one dime. I stole clothes and food, and my mother would protest. I would feed my brothers while she was at work. In fact, I used to steal potato chips from this very building we are in right now, Happy's Potato Chip factory.

My mother finally gave in to my criminal lifestyle as there was nothing she could do about it. I was mad at her for not fighting back at my dad, and I just went my own way. By then there were six of us boys in the family, and then, after my parents got back together for a short period of time, my little sister came along. By now it's the 1970s and I'm eighteen and running the streets with all kinds of angry young men who saw themselves as part of the Black Power movement.

About this time my cousin Tommy was killed. I had been in an argument with a lady down the street, and she threw a handful of lye in my face. I ran down the street to my aunt's house where Tommy lived and she put some type of milk on my face that diluted the lye. Tommy asked what happened and he went down to the other house to settle things up, and they shot him in the chest with a shotgun. He died defending me, and that was hard for me to live with because I had been the agitator.

Nobody messed with my younger brothers as they knew I would retaliate in force. My nickname was Taz, named for the Tasmanian Devil. In the County Home School I was a problem inmate because I threatened the staff. Finally they wouldn't accept me anymore as I was too unpredictable. I figured if I was tough enough people wouldn't mess with me. During this time I had no positive male influences. When I was fourteen there was this coach that my friend Jimmy and I would visit for a sleepover. I always knew there was something wrong so we never went over there alone. He had a roommate named Pete who didn't like us. It was like they were a couple. The coach used to have us sleep in the bed with him and would take pictures once in a while as we were going to sleep. He was later indicted for having thousands of pictures of child pornography.

There were simply no male figures around to look out for us, so we wound up working the streets.

My first child was born when I was sixteen years old. The birth was unusual. My girlfriend was nine months pregnant when I got into an argument with a guy; it turned violent and I came out on top. I just forgot about it and sat down with my girlfriend to watch TV—I was getting high. The guy came back downstairs and my girlfriend saw him and jumped up. Just as I turned I heard his gun go off and she started screaming. I looked over at the guy, he was still pointing the gun at me but the barrel had dropped after the gunshot so I instinctively ran towards him. By this time I knew about guns, though I wasn't carrying one—mine was hidden up in the rafters. I had been shot in the arm, but I thought my girlfriend was OK until we headed upstairs and I realized she'd been shot in her belly. The ambulance came, and that night my daughter was born, so all three of us were in the hospital at the same time. Somehow the bullet had missed my daughter—that was God—and that's how she came into this world. So at the age of seventeen I was a dad and also basically a criminal.

My girlfriend was a year older than me, and she was able to get on welfare. I was now a dad living on food stamps in an apartment that had the rent paid. All I had to do was make some extra money, and I did that through armed robbery. I had some very ugly armed robbery experiences where people got hurt. I went to prison when I was nineteen for aggravated robbery, aggravated assault, home invasion, and stuff like that. Most of the crimes I committed took place at shops in our neighborhood along Lake Street in south Minneapolis. That was my line of business, and I usually worked by myself. By then I had been introduced to gangs but didn't like the concept because I didn't want another man to be in charge of my life. But in prison I got to start my own. It was called the Black Brotherhood Cultural Development Organization. With eighty gang members I ran that prison for three and a half years. We controlled prostitution, drugs, living arrangements, how they did their time, phone calls, and we bought and sold anything anybody wanted. I kept power by supplying the five guys that worked for me. They were all in for murder.

During my stay there I ran into a guard named John. He was one of the most hated guards in the penitentiary, but for some reason he liked me. He said I had leadership potential. John started a mentoring program and brought in people from the outside to talk to us. I respected him as the police because he did his job well, and he respected me for my influence inside. I respected him enough to never try to buy him off. Here I was, a nineteen-year-old kid with a few guards and several inmates working for me. I had more management headaches than many big-time executives.

But the most important thing was that while in prison I couldn't raise my daughter. I wasn't there for her. Not long after I got out, my son, Johnny, was born at Methodist Hospital. I was high, and they kicked me out of the hospital for stealing something. My behavior was despicable. Financially I always took care of my kids, but I was never around for them. My wife was alcoholic and I was on drugs much of the time. We had three kids together: Lisa, Johnny, and Jamie. I had walked away from all religious teaching, all value systems, at the age of twelve, so God had no role in my life.

I first met Art Erickson, the founder of this place called Urban Ventures Leadership Foundation, when I was eighteen. He was always around in the neighborhood, urging young people to go to school. We may have met at his food shelf. At the time I had no need for that kind of friendship. I had been kicked out of the public schools when I was seventeen. I was kicked out of Central High for carrying a gun. The assistant principal said something to me that I didn't like, and I had some very choice words for him. I was permanently suspended from the public schools.

I finally got my GED at the Red Wing reformatory for boys. I was a leader there. At this time they started a thing with a Catholic priest named Father Capuchi. He really liked me and could get me to calm down. In Red Wing they first put you in cells naked and if you were nice you got a piss bucket. You did that for about ten days before moving to a regular cell. Father Capuchi was the only one who would come in there with us. He loved us, and we could tell. We really respected him greatly.

I got my GED because I wanted to learn how to do power weight-lifting. Mr. Drews taught us. He was one of the power weightlifting champions in Minnesota. He told me that the only way he would teach me weightlifting was if I got my GED. While in solitary confinement I studied, took the tests, and passed them all the first time.

I got married when I was in prison so that I could have conjugal visits. That was the only reason I got married. By this time I had had another son by another woman. His name is Shawn. I was with him for a year and a half. I was in prison when this guy was babysitting him and Shawn was beaten to death. My wife had run off with the guy. She was a prostitute who would set up tricks to be robbed and that sort of thing. She would set them up and I would rob them. We ran a pretty successful business. After this guy killed my son, a preacher helped me get out to go to the funeral.

At that time, when I was in my twenties, I became suicidal. I wanted someone to kill me or else I wanted to have a drug overdose. The only thing that kept me from pulling the plug was that I didn't want to let my family down. In prison I never did drugs; I just sold them. It didn't make sense. They cost too much. Something that might cost a dollar on the street could be twenty dollars in jail. So I made a lot of money in prison controlling drug flows.

At that time I signed up for an Amicus volunteer. The word means "friend," and the organization trained volunteers to visit and counsel inmates. They sent a college professor to me, and he was very engaging. He thought I was smart and should go back to school. He just kept at that...so I did.

I went to school for computer programming. I caught on easily and became one of the best programmers in Stillwater prison. When I got out I got a job as a programmer. So I had been at Glen Lake Home School, then graduated to Red Wing. Twice I was in the "work house" and from there I went to B building at Lino Lakes, which is where they put young guys headed for prison who were violent and crazy. My next stop was the prison at St. Cloud, and then two times in Stillwater in my late twenties.

During those later tours I became more interested in education. My need to be violent and hard was fading away, so I entered a long-term treatment program. My Amicus volunteer was the only person who came to see me other than my wife, who came once so we could have sex. She wound up in prison herself and eventually died of an overdose.

I have been married five times. I have always believed in marriage. Unfortunately, I didn't marry the mother of my first child. More unfortunately, I didn't know how to be a husband. While I had good intentions, a drug addict and thief don't make a good husband. A man who knows little, is very violent, and doesn't accept Christ doesn't make a good husband. There were times when my wives loved me and I loved them, but I didn't make a good husband. The women I chose were also into drugs, and that's a bad combination for a marriage. It just doesn't work.

I always had this pull to go back to church, but I just couldn't give up the other stuff. We had a lot of family members who all settled in the same area south of Lake Street in Minneapolis. My son, along with a number of his little cousins, started their own gang. It was called the Bloods, and we always taught that if you attacked one of us you attacked us all. So it was really a family gang. We were known as being very violent and destructive.

My mother and the women in the family all went to church. We didn't. In my dad's family there were twelve and in my mom's eighteen. We were a very large family. My mother's family name was Dower. The Dowers were educated. The Turnipseeds were not. The Dowers went to college and the Turnipseeds went to jail.

I knew that God existed and at times I cried out to him, but the pull of the streets was too strong. The power that I had was too intoxicating. At one time I had eight girlfriends who all knew each other. Drugs, crack cocaine, and heroin were my other companions. My kids have always loved me. I have always felt love for my kids. Somehow they knew that. For some reason they loved me in spite of the fact that I abandoned them most of the time. I never mistreated my daughters or spanked the boys. At this time little Johnny was growing up trying to be a bigger version of me. He idolized me and took my evil to another level. He became one of the most hated African American kids in Minnesota.

If you Google "Lil Johnny Edwards" you'll find at least twenty articles about him. He was shot seventeen times and the police hated him. His own family doesn't like him, and he is in prison now for his own protection. When he was shot the second time it took his leg off. I was in prison at the time and made a deal with God. I told him that I would walk away from drugs, pimping, and the gangs if Lil Johnny lived. He lived, so I was trapped.

I walked away from all of that, got sober, and stopped carrying a gun, but my character hadn't changed.

Two years after I made that deal with God I got a job teaching computer programming at Resource Inc., a non-profit that prepares people for living-wage jobs. We taught a number of disabled students. I was very good at adapting equipment to students with disabilities. One of my best students was legally blind and became one of my teachers. He taught Windows and Excel without ever seeing the screen. It was amazing.

Then I was arrested! A police task force had been looking for me. I ran a group of computer thieves who stole parts in Minnesota and sold them in Wisconsin, stole parts in Wisconsin and sold them in St. Louis. I used guys who knew about computer memory chips. We would go into businesses on Saturdays, bypass the alarm system, and remove the memory from the computer, put the cover back on and then take off. It had to be frustrating for the workers when they came back to the office and tried to turn their machines on. It took only three minutes to get the chip out, though it was worth $200 on the street. The police formed a task force and within a few weeks they caught me.

I had been laid up with a hernia operation but could hobble around and run my people by telephone. It was a particularly difficult job the guys were on. I went out and checked out these two buildings we were going to rob. Sometimes when we went in I would crack the safe and take the money so investigators would think that's what we were after. We always wore suits and looked liked business people as we walked out with memory chips tucked into hidden pockets we'd sewn into our suits. We looked very businesslike.

Unfortunately, the Edina police and other suburban forces were watching me twenty-four/seven and caught me in the act. I didn't give up any of my friends but took the whole rap myself. I was sentenced to forty years! An aggressive crime reporter named Tom Lyden from Channel 9 news followed the case.

At the time I was arrested I had been trying to change my life and had once again run into Art Erickson, the man who founded Urban Ventures Leadership Foundation. Art had always been around my neighborhood. Because I wanted to get back together with my kids I joined this "fathering program" he ran. I was thirty-nine years old, had quit using drugs, was a good teacher, always wore suits, and had good communication skills. My one black mark was the computer-memory theft business I was running on the side. There were weeks when I made $20,000. I was trying to do the right thing but really didn't know how and had never asked God to help me. it was about nine months after I joined the program that I got busted and the walls came tumbling down.

Criminal lifestyles are very addictive. There is a lot of risk involved, but there are also high rewards and a lot of intellectual satisfaction. I'm not talking about local neighborhood stick-ups. What we did required careful planning, good communication, and discipline. I never carried a weapon. By this time the police had sort of forgotten about me. It seemed that after eight previous felony convictions and time spent in nearly every prison in Minnesota, I had turned my back on violence and adopted a normal, drug-free lifestyle. More than thirty family members were in jail for murder, including my grandson, who is serving a life sentence without the chance of parole. Many of my relatives had watched me and picked up my bad habits. So I joined this fathering program hoping to make a difference. These kids either didn't have a father at home, or if they did, he was crooked and a bad role model.

So I'm in the fathering program, teaching at Resource, Inc., and then I get busted. And it's all on TV! My family members in prison called to congratulate me for being in the news. They were really proud of me for making it big time. Everybody else walked away from me, saying "I told you so." They charged me with fifty counts, and I pleaded guilty and said that I would take them all.

I was so disgusted that I had let my children down. Because I pleaded guilty, the Edina police let me finish teaching at Resource, Inc. for six months after the trial. I was teaching Cobalt, which was still in use at the time with large mainframe computers. There were very few who could still program and teach Cobalt at that time. That computer language hasn't changed since 1974. Resource had made a commitment to these students to maintain the course, and I was the only one who could teach it.

The only attorney who would help me at a price I could afford was Jerod Peterson, who had previously been with the Legal Rights Center. I had used Jerod before when I was busted for stealing computers. The mistake I made then was to steal a computer with a signal that automatically told the owner where it was unless you blocked that signal. My kids got on the computer and the police busted into my home within the hour.

Jerod liked me for some reason, maybe because I was always dressed up in court and made a good impression. Sometimes they thought I was one of the attorneys. He required $500 up front, which I had, and put me on a payment plan. Perhaps he thought I might be a good advertisement for his law practice. I told Jerod that I had joined the fathering program and was teaching at Resource. He went to bat for me, as did Art Erickson, who immediately came to my defense.

Art knew my whole family. He knew about my criminal lifestyle. He didn't ask any questions but just offered to help. Art was an ordained minister, and I hadn't turned my life over to Christ at that time. Here is how I did.

I was teaching in my school after the conviction, but my students weren't aware that I was a criminal until the news guy tracked me down. They told me that the press was downstairs. I remember looking at my students and then telling my boss about the deal I'd made with the police. I went up to my office and was so ashamed, I locked the door and began to weep. I couldn't stop crying. I had let everybody down—my family and my students and others who believed in me. I'd gotten off drugs and changed my life, but was still dabbling in crime to feed my gambling habit.

The first thing I did between tears was to call my mother. Here I am at age thirty-nine calling my mother. Mom told me to take my life to Jesus and that's what I did. I asked God to take over my life. My prayers were to accept my punishment and then be able to teach again some day and have my kids still love me. So when Art Erickson came to visit me I told him the whole story of what I had been…all of it! He invited me to his office, gave me biblical verses to read, and told me that we were all sinners in one way or another. It's just that some of us are lucky and don't get caught. These were some basic things that I needed to hear.

Jerod Peterson kept working hard on my case and succeeded

in whittling my sentence down to ten years, so I would be fifty when I got out. I was just lucky that the feds never got on to me because our computer memory theft business was an act of interstate commerce. If they'd found out I would never have seen daylight again. At the last moment Jerod got the judge to reduce my sentence to eighty-six months. That was eighty-six months for a three-time loser with fifty felonies! Judge Gary Larson for some reason felt that there were still some redeeming qualities left in my shattered life.

So now I'm feeling pretty good and I could see the end of this, because with good behavior I would serve only two thirds of the sentence and be out in about five years. On the last day in court, with Art Erickson pulling for me and Jesus Christ sitting on my shoulder and helping Jerod Peterson, Judge Larson changed his mind. He decided he didn't want me to go to prison, and gave me two years consecutive in the work house with work release privileges so I could still teach. Immediately God had answered my one prayer about teaching. The school not only let me keep my job, but they promoted me. I was now the lead instructor running the whole program with people with PhDs working under me! Deborah Atterberry was executive director of Resource at the time. After ninety days at the work house the judge let me out on house arrest.

I saw Judge Larson about two years ago. He had tears in his eyes because he was so glad that I'd changed my life and helped others these past twenty years. He had taken a chance on me and it had paid off. Judge Larson is my hero, and to this day I don't know what he saw in me that made him change his mind. You see, I was being prosecuted by the career criminal division of Hennepin County. When they show up, you are in trouble. One of the toughest of the lot had my case. He had prosecuted my son and cousins for murder, and he felt we were the most despicable family on the planet. One thing that helped was that Art Erickson told the judge that he would give me a job if they released me. All this happened to me by the grace of God.

I have now been teaching at Urban Ventures Leadership Foundation for nineteen years! I've been director of the Center for Fathering for fifteen years. The other great thing that happened was that I got reunited with my kids. I had asked God for that, and he not only reunited me with my kids but he brought back to me two that I didn't even know existed. Another positive thing is that I just got custody of my great-grandson, who was living in a crack house. So the family thing has finally come together for me.

You might think I'm saying that if you turn your life over to Christ then everything works out. Not so. The police were very angry that I'd gotten this break, and three years later I was arrested when six people claimed they saw me at the scene of a crime. Art Erickson again came to my defense. My alibis were solid, as I was with former Governor Quie on one of the occasions they claimed I was committing a crime. We found out later there was a copycat kid in town emulating my former life. So finally the harassment stopped and God had truly protected me. For me my life has been miraculous!

My last marriage has lasted now for eight years. I have always believed in the sanctity of marriage and never played around when I was married. In between marriages I just went wild. My daughters are doing very well, and the boys other than Johnny are doing fine. I have now done things I never believed were possible. I have met with the Dalai Lama, Colin Powell, Al Quie, and other established leaders.

The fathering program here is based on character

development. It's different from other fathering programs. We don't exactly teach fathering as a first step. We talk to men about role modeling, drug abuse, and domestic abuse first, because to become a good father, you must first become a good man. If you can't overcome your violent tendencies, you might as well have Satan in the house because he's a provider too! We tell men that if they don't change, these fathering classes won't mean a thing.

They hear about the program in several ways. I go to the prisons and jails and make the usual rounds. However, a lot of them hear about us on the bus lines. We send five or six guys out a day to ride the city buses. We talk to the troublemakers on the buses. We approach guys standing on the street corners and tell our story. Much of this evolved from a group we helped start called Mad Dads. One of the guys that runs our local Mad Dads chapter is now head of the national organization. He came through our fathering program. We reach into these men and pull the best out of them. Our greatest tool is the love of Jesus Christ. There are four facilitators and me in the program. We spend a lot of time simply teaching men how they can live with their families and have a meaningful relationship. We're now the largest such program in the country. I graduate about four hundred men a year, contact roughly a thousand on the streets, and see as many as two thousand in the jails.

Looking back, I think what happened to my dad was that he lost his support base. We all went to church, there were other families that supported one another, and he was in a disciplined and controlled environment. I don't know how all that broke down when he came up to Minnesota alone. I can only specu- late. Somehow he had lost his support system. Obviously my father had a negative influence on me, as did my cousin Tommy, who helped protect my mom but otherwise was a terrible influence. In retrospect, the Black Panther movement was not a good influence. On the other hand, in addition to Art Erickson, I was also helped in my transformation by Dave Roth, who directed the training program at Resource, Inc. My grandmother and the rest of my family, including my father, were wonderful influences for me when we lived in Alabama.

With respect to the future, I believe if we do not begin to focus on the family structure we will never eliminate the crime and violence and social breakdown that plague our communities. We as a nation have walked away from the family structure. One good family is worth more than five good social organizations. If the older brother and sister are strong as well as the parents in a family, with a belief system that includes spiritual values and where the parents rather than the truant officer gets the kids off to school, then we have a chance. Kids need someone around who loves them. If we can get back to those ideals, then there is hope!

So Urban Ventures is the right place for me. It focuses on the family. We find guys who are connected to the streets. They, in turn, can recruit others not connected because they have credibility.

Let me explain something. You can be in the toughest gang community that is all black. Then all of a sudden two well-dressed white guys on very nice bicycles show up and they are never harmed. They are Mormons. The reason they are never harmed is because they are God's boys and they get a pass. They were perfect victims, but we never robbed them or stole their bikes because we had the fear of who they served. That's why a minister or priest or nun can walk through the toughest of communities and not be harmed. It's built into their DNA that people of God are respected and protected. You just rarely hear of truly religious church people being harmed. Now if they see a hypocrite in you, then that's a different story.

The neighborhood that brought John Turnipseed and Art Erickson together is immediately south of what is now the home of Wells Fargo's mortgage business. Previously it was the site of Honeywell. In the 1940s and 1950s, Lake Street had been the heart of automobile and farm implement sales and a host of manufacturing and service businesses. With the flight to the suburbs in the 1970s and 1980s the area lost much of its business and civic leadership. For years this neighborhood had lacked a decent support system for kids. Prostitution and drugs were common on Lake Street, which is the central corridor running through the area. Through the leadership of Art Erickson, who for years was a youth minister in the area, Urban Ventures was founded and has brought a renewed sense of hope and vitality to the area. With a focus on both youth and economic development, Urban Ventures has been a significant factor in the turn-around of both the Lake Street corridor and the surrounding neighborhoods. Art Erickson lives and works there. There are still occasional drive-by shootings, and street crime persists, but overall life has substantially improved for the residents and new businesses are reenergizing the economy. This was not the case when John Turnipseed grew up there in the 1960s.

Ashley Bath

"My dad tried to strangle me with a telephone cord one night and later knocked me out in the bath tub ... Minnesota's treatment program for young people like me was key to my life turnaround. Affordable housing got me off the streets and into a safe environment. Food stamps and food shelves were also essential for keeping my diet healthy."

This young woman survived a perfect storm of abuse and neglect and is now self-sufficient and giving back. Her odyssey of bouncing from place to place, attempting to find a safe harbor, led to drug abuse, which made her even more vulnerable to predators. Were it not for a straight-talking grandmother and a devoted not-for-profit counselor, Ashley would likely not be with us today. This is a disturbing story but fortunately one with a hopeful ending.

My name is Ashley Bath. I was born in Coon Rapids, Minnesota. My parents moved to Seattle early on, and I later moved back to Minnesota with my brother and stayed with my grandparents. My grandparents raised me off and on throughout my very early life. We lived in several different places during those early years, shuttling between parents and grandparents in Anoka, Arden Hills, and St. Francis.

My parents divorced when I was nine. My dad was an

alcoholic, abusive and neglectful. Often he didn't come home for weeks at a time. We didn't have heat in the winter. My brother and I pretty much raised ourselves, as my mom was off being single again. By then my grandparents had moved up north to Deerwood, Minnesota, so they were no longer close by, though we still felt like they were raising us psychologically. My mom had left us so we had to stay with my dad. He met a woman, my best friend's mom. She was really abusive to me, sometimes laying me on the ground and beating on me. My dad assaulted my brother so he moved back in with my mom. From then on, I pretty much really raised myself.

My seventh grade teacher, Mr. King, was worried about what was going on at my home, and he got the local child protection people involved. Somehow my dad heard that they were coming, cleaned up the house, and threatened to kill me if I ever told what was really going on. So when they arrived, Anoka County Services saw what appeared to be one big happy family.

Yet it seemed like the police were out at our house every week for one reason or another. Nobody really believed me; they all thought I was just a kid being behavioral. Well, you don't become behavioral for no reason! My dad tried to strangle me with a telephone cord one night and later knocked me out in the bathtub. He was just an abusive asshole...that's the best way to put it. I ended up getting into drugs and alcohol, sneaking out of the house by the time I was twelve, and stuff like that. I would get into fights at school. I just really did not care about anything. I even ended up in the psych ward at Abbott Northwestern Hospital for cutting my wrists after overdosing on pills. They popped me full of medication, but nobody ever really dealt with the core issue: I was not being taken care of. To help a young person like me, someone has to take time out to listen to what you have to say. There is so much stuff bottled up inside, and it has to be released before a patient can begin to regain their health. Medication just makes things worse. I was resentful that I had to be on it, nobody listened, and no one would take me outside of the house. I did move in with my mom briefly in fifth grade, after my parents had split up. My behavior became destructive because I often didn't believe that my mom was actually coming home. I worried that I would be left alone. She eventually kicked me out of the house and I went back with my dad, which was no help at all—just another part of my downward spiral. Being a young girl and not having your mom is a big deal. Just thinking about it now is causing me to choke up.

I went to counseling for many weeks, and they would ask, "What about your mom?" I couldn't talk about her and went for months not mentioning her name. It was like she didn't really exist. My cutting continued and I was back in the psych ward at ages thirteen and fourteen. When your body is so numb that you don't feel anything, that's when cutting starts. You have forgotten how to feel anything. You have forgotten how to address simple emotions so you just shut everything down. When you do cut yourself you feel alive again because you can say to yourself, "This really hurts." While it sounds strange, this cutting of one's skin is very releasing.

My older brother was no help, and through it all he blamed me for the dysfunction in our family. The last time my dad hit me I was seventeen, and I returned the blows and knocked him out cold. I had had enough and was not going to take it anymore. He has never laid a hand on me since! I won't tolerate that from anyone anymore. There is a reason why kids act up, but most of the time no one wants to hear about it. The problem psychologists had with me was that I was very intelligent and advanced for my age, and they just didn't want to listen to what I understood about myself.

My school during those years was Sobriety High in Burnsville. I wanted to stay sober and graduate after years of smoking pot and using alcohol. After I got my driver's license I felt a new sense of freedom, started using drugs again, and got involved with a boy. There was an episode where I thought my mom's boyfriend was going to push my mom down the stairs so I knocked him out. They ended up calling the cops and I was arrested in the Walmart parking lot near my mom's house in Shakopee. They put me in a juvenile detention house for three weeks, and then I had to take an anger management treatment program for five months in Eau Claire, Wisconsin. That place was like jail. There were rapist children there, anorexic kids, bulimic youth, and delinquent kids that could not be housed anyplace else. It was just a holding tank for dysfunctional kids. In there one forgets how to live in society. There is no such thing as the outside world. It is a terrible adjustment coming back out when it's over. You just become totally institutionalized.

Eventually I was released, moved back in with my dad, and went back to school. I started smoking pot again, dropped out of high school, and started working because my dad wanted me to pay rent. He was still drunk much of the time and would have sex in front of me with girls he brought back from the bar. He would hit on my friends and was just such an unhealthy person. This was so wrong. I escaped by using drugs like Ecstasy, which has a euphoric affect on you. After dropping out of high school I did take a class on alcoholism, and I leaned about neurotransmitters and the science of what drugs do to you. I wanted to know everything there was to know about the brain and how these chemicals affected it.

My story is sort of chopped up because there's so much I'm trying to remember. At age seventeen I left home and stayed with friends, house hopped, and eventually moved up to Deerwood to live with my grandparents again. My grandfather was alcoholic so we wound up drinking together. I was very abusive to my grandparents emotionally. My brother came there with his girlfriend that he'd gotten pregnant, we got in a fight, and I said some things that I now deeply regret. I left and moved in with my aunt, who lived nearby. Then I started talking to some guy online, as I wanted to get out of there. He was forty and I had just turned eighteen. We met, and before long I was back on drugs and now using cocaine. He took videos of us doing sex that I was not aware of. He stole my birth certificate and driver's license and tied me up and abused me. I finally put all my stuff in garbage bags and was in the process of moving out when he came after me again. I called the police, and he is now in jail. That night I stayed in the park, then cleaned up in the local library, stayed with a friend in a group home the next day, and finally called my other grandparents—my mom's mom—and moved in with them.

My grandmother picked me up. She was very direct with me, asking me what I wanted as a future. She told me that no one worthwhile would want me, that I was damaged goods and would have no future unless I cleaned up my act. I was so insulted and angry. Now I realize that she was right. If you don't love yourself, how will anyone else ever love you? If you don't take pride in the things you do and who you are, no one will ever respect you. She talked to my mom, and then she told me that if I didn't go to treatment that very day, no one in the family would ever have anything to do with me again. I checked to see if Minnesota's insurance program [Rule 25] for addicts like me would cover the cost. It did, so I entered treatment at Tapestry. I was there for a month. Minnesota really does a good job of giving addicts the tools to survive.

Since August 28, 2008, I have been clean from cocaine. I did have one episode where I almost killed myself and overdosed on some pills I had held on to. I called the ambulance and would have died if they hadn't treated me. I told them it was an accident and that I really didn't want to kill myself, and I was released from the hospital. I stayed with my dad briefly until I could get into a halfway house. It was the Gables in Rochester, Minnesota. I arranged that all on my own. I have now moved a total of twenty-nine times in my lifetime.

After leaving the Gables I moved in with my boyfriend's family, then back with my mom for three months, and then to a homeless shelter for four months. Someone in Alcoholics Anonymous gifted me a car so I was able to get around and got a job in retail. I moved several more times and finally heard about Lincoln Place, which is in Eagan, Minnesota. I had no social worker to refer me so I was their only self-referral. They took me because I'd been diagnosed as having mental issues. It's affordable housing for young people who are homeless. A non-profit called The Link runs Lincoln Place and Dakota County funds it. I stayed there from April 1, 2010, to October 31, 2011. That's how I met Carrie Yeager, who is an employment counselor with HIRED, one of the region's largest managers of job skill training programs. I still stay in touch with Carrie. She is helping me get funding for college. I want to go to Colorado Technical University. It costs about $50,000 for a four-year degree.

At HIRED Ashley participated in their comprehensive job search training program. Carrie helped her assess her skills

and job interests. She learned how to complete an application, network, interview, and work on her job-retention skills. With Carrie's assistance, she earned her forklift operator credentials and then interned as a volunteer aide at the Eagan Community Center, working with senior citizens. At that time Ashley decided to focus on a career in human services.

The only reason I was able to go to school at all was because of Anna Judge, a property manager for Dakota County. I attended one semester at Normandale Community College and then was accepted at Naropa University in Colorado, but I have yet to put the financing together. I worked at a restaurant for a while and then started at an online school called Kaplan. I was getting all As but couldn't find the funding to continue. Carrie stuck with me as I tried to find work. I got a call back from Options Residential, had an interview, and was hired. Now I worked for Options as a resource counselor in a group home called Metropolitan Living, serving people with brain injuries, mental illness, and addiction. We help clients with independent-living skills like cooking, taking showers, and medical care. We also teach aggression replacement therapy and other communication and life skills.

So now I'm on the other side—teaching what I experienced in my own life. Life is now good, I have my own apartment, and I'm putting some money away for school. I have had a relationship with a very good man, but I now know that I'm not ready for a serious relationship. I need to work on myself for now and prepare wisely for the future.

Now that I have my own apartment, car, cell phone, and insurance, it feels very good. There is now no such thing as a bad day. Each day is a new learning experience. My current goal is to get back to school in Colorado by next year.

Thinking back on it, there were a number of things that helped me get back on my feet. Moving to a smaller school helped, as large schools can be very stressful when you're trying to free yourself from chemical and drug addiction. And Minnesota's treatment program for young people like me was key to my life turnaround. Affordable housing got me off the streets and into a safe environment. Food stamps and food shelves were also essential for keeping my diet healthy. But too much social support can be as harmful as too little, I think. You can destroy incentive with the wrong kind of support. There is a program called GRH [Group Residential Housing] that I think encourages dependency. Tough love is the key. The balance is what is essential. If the system provides the tools, then it's up to us to make the rest happen.

I owe a lot to Carrie and all the others who have been so helpful to me. She found me housing, gave me gas cards, helped me get my GED, encouraged me, and gave me little rewards like Target cards for making progress. This helped me set goals and learn that there can be rewards for reaching them. Carrie found me work at volunteer internships that gave me needed social and work experience and also boosted my confidence and self-esteem. I even got a modest paycheck so I could develop good financial habits. All these things had to be in place before she could help me find work. HIRED does an amazing job not only of preparing you for work, but also of helping you land a job when you're ready for one. They also stay with you after you start work to make sure you don't mess up.

There were several times when I let Carrie down but she never gave up on me. Her attitude was "I'm not here to judge you. I'm here to help you. Now where do we go from here?" She was the friend that was always there. I probably would not have made it without Carrie and HIRED. Her motto is, "I can walk across the finish line with you, but I can't carry you."

How adults can develop such destructive parenting skills as Ashley's mother and father exhibited is a mystery to me. I can only suspect that a lack of education, poor self-esteem, financial stress, and their own abusive role models may all be contributing factors. One of the key lessons from Ashley's story is the way the system sometimes works to treat the symptoms and not the root causes of the damaged emotions that underlie addictive behavior. While not necessarily an explicit motive, there is money to be made and time to be saved on the front end by medicating people who have addictive issues, as opposed to treating the causes of their addiction. The pain and social costs later in life more than offset these short-term savings, but they're paid by someone else. The tough love offered by people like Carrie was likely the best therapy Ashley could have had, and most likely was the key to her gaining a new life.

Cherkos Dessalegn

"Kids from poor families don't receive that all-important push. It is a compliment to the school when kids get into a great college or university and it also helps the school's ratings. But what about the others—the 25 percent who with encouragement and mentoring could also have a shot at a future."

We recently took our twelve-year-old grandchild on a trip to New York, where we spent much of one morning at Ellis Island. I thought of Cherkos while we learned of the challenges faced by immigrants in the early years of immigration to the United States, and how similar the barriers might have been for Cherkos and his family in 2001. In addition to the emotional hardship of leaving one's homeland and settling in a new country, the cultural and language barriers must have been immense, regardless of the era. I suspect our support system for refugees is more effective today, and that for the well-educated, technology may permit more rapid advancement economically. Nevertheless, as Cherkos tells his story, it becomes clear that the racism experienced by newcomers, especially those of color, persists. What is most interesting to me are Cherkos's keen observations about what needs to be done to improve our large public education systems.

I was born in the northern part of Ethiopia in 1986. The year I was born, the civil war was going on and my dad had to get out of the country for political reasons. He settled in a refugee camp in Sudan, came to America in the early 1990s, and settled in Minnesota. My mom and we five children were still in Ethiopia and came here in 2001.We lived in St. Paul, and I attended Highland Park High School as a freshman. This was a difficult adjustment, and I worked hard in class to prove myself. Because Ethiopia was never colonized, we never had to learn a foreign language, so this was all a new experience for my siblings and me. I grew up speaking Tigrigna, which is common in the northern part of the country, and also spoke Amharic, the national language in Ethiopia. Luckily we had a large group of Ethiopian students at Highland Park.

In my sophomore year, I saw a flyer on the bulletin board at school. It told about Admission Possible [now College Possible] and how they could help one go to college. I was sixteen years old at the time, and most of my friends were not thinking about college. We were all into soccer and basketball and just hanging out, but I decided to check it out. I went downstairs and met their representative, who was called a coach, and she went over the program with me. It was all new to me. My parents, though pro education, had no knowledge of college or how one might get there or pay for it. I was the fourth in my family, but my two older sisters hadn't gone to college because there was no one there to show them how to do it. Seeing that, I wanted a different future for myself. The program sounded pretty awesome. I registered, and during my junior year we started doing the college access program, ACT, and ACT Prep. In order to make this work I had to cut back on sports as I was overly involved in almost everything.

My motivation, in part, was seeing how hard both my parents worked, with my dad holding down two jobs trying to care for our family. With five kids and being in a new community, my dad was everywhere for us. He worked at Chili's restaurant as a cook and also as a janitor at Minneapolis-St. Paul International Airport. It was strange at the time, because I had many teachers helping me out once they learned that I had college in mind. There were also a few who, for some reason, told me I was not suited for college. I am not the kind of person who lets anyone break me down so I wound up getting a lot of help and doing well. My parents raised us to believe that it doesn't matter how bad it is or how hard it is...just do your best in every way. They pushed us to the limit. During my freshman year I took English as a second language; in the second half of my sophomore year I was enrolled in honor classes, and the next year in International Baccalaureate classes! My College Possible coach was always there for me. We still keep in touch and are good friends.

Senior year I started the college process. I applied to the University of Minnesota, the University of Minnesota–Duluth, Mankato State, and Southwest University in Marshall, Minnesota, and was accepted at all four! The U of M was my first choice. When I looked at the financial aid package I had to make a different choice.

The Schwan Food Company is located in Marshall, Minnesota, and has been promoting more diversity at Southwest U. At the time there were very few students of color attending there. My coach at College Possible was aware of their scholarship program and said that because of my GPA and ACT scores, I was eligible. She told me that if I applied and was successful, I could pretty much go to college for free. Knowing how many other students finished college heavily in debt, I was averse to taking out loans, so I wrote the required essay, completed all the paperwork, and soon afterward received a phone call saying I was among ten finalists for scholarships among the forty-five who had applied. I was asked to come down for an interview.

It was so rewarding to see the excitement in Cherkos's expression as he related how he felt when this incredible opportunity fell into his lap. For those of us born here into comfortable circumstances, with families who could afford to send us to college, it's a reminder of how incredibly fortunate many of us are. It's also a tribute to Schwan Food Company, whose support reflects some of the very best in corporate philanthropy. The path Cherkos had chosen would not be easy, however, as he and other participants in the scholarship program were among the first young men to bring diversity to Marshall, Minnesota, in much the same way that African American youth of the early 1960s had struggled to integrate the American South.

That fall was my first experience in a rural agricultural area. It both looked and smelled different than St. Paul. It's difficult to convey how different that rural culture was for a boy who was used to living where there was diversity in the community. The adjustment in coming to America and learning the language was hard enough. This was something else again, as we stood out so clearly among the local folks. My College Possible coach had warned me that there would be people who were afraid of young men like me, whose appearance and speech differed from local norms. Naturally the ten of us in the program hung out together because we shared the same background, and in a way it was our small group and then the other three thousand students and one hundred faculty members.

The first year was hard, but my coach continued to call and tell me to suck it up and hang in there. I was also motivated to succeed for my family. After the first year, five of our group of ten dropped out. Only three of us graduated within the traditional four years. The main reason students gave for dropping out had little to do with academic issues. It was because of how they felt they were being treated. On one occasion we visited a mini-mall, and many of the local folks just took off at a fast pace when they saw us coming. Just like that, they separated from us. We could not relate to their fear, and it made us feel both unwanted and scared.

Many of the students in the program were also working full time and received additional support from their parents. Eventually most found other schools and finished their degree programs, but it often took eight years. Of the original high school group that was with me in my local College Possible program, only one finished at a local community college; the rest wound up doing odd jobs. Every time they see me now they regret that they did not follow up with College Possible.

During my last three years at Marshall, I worked thirty-six hours a week at a group home for mentally disabled persons. It was gratifying to be helping people, and my manager was an awesome guy who understood our situation. My job was to remind clients to take their meds and get to their medical appointments, and beyond that, help them entertain themselves. I still hear from some of these folks. They taught me a lot about myself and life in general.

Schwan's also had an internship program that I participated in for three summers, which taught me a lot about business finance, sales, and production. As a young kid I was hanging out with the CFO and even flew with him on the corporate jet. These guys were mentors to me. It was a good feeling to sense that they believed in me, that I could accomplish things, and that I had a future in front of me. It motivated me to work harder in school.

Before graduation in 2010, I started looking for a job. I attended a job fair at the Minneapolis Convention Center put on by the Minnesota Colleges and University System. Wells Fargo had a booth, and the regional manager gave me his card. I put it on my door so I could see it every day. One night I sat down and for the first time tried to figure out how to market myself. I sent him an email and he replied the next day! They offered me a position as an assistant to the credit manager. The problem was that it was in a relatively small town in South Dakota, about two hours from Sioux Falls. I told him that I had already spent four years in Marshall, a relatively small town, and I didn't want to go through that again. Unfortunately, they didn't have a position open in a larger community like Sioux Falls, Mankato, or the Twin Cities.

As I drove back to campus from the interview, it occurred to me that during my academic career my coach at College Possible had helped me more than anyone else. Maybe I could get a job there?

College Possible has more than four hundred applicants a year for their job openings. They accept only about forty for final interviews. When I used to come home from Marshall to visit my parents, I would walk the old neighborhood and see kids in trouble or just hanging out with no sense of direction. When I talked to them they would tell me they didn't know what to do or couldn't get along in school—stuff like that. I began to ask myself what I could do to help give these kids a better shot at life. I remembered the many calls and emails I got from my

College Possible coaches while at Southwest, asking if I needed help with academics or financial assistance or writing a resume, or if nothing else, then just giving me encouragement. They did this throughout the four years I was there. I filled out an application to College Possible one day before the deadline. Since I was still at Marshall, and there was no way my application could get there in time by mail, the next morning I woke early, drove to the Twin Cities head office, and dropped off the application personally. It was 10:30 a.m.—ninety minutes before the deadline. I then drove the three hours back to Marshall because I had a class in business policy that night.

Two weeks later I was invited to come for an interview. One month later they told me that I could join their program. They thought I could be a good coach. I told them that my one condition was that they place me at my old school, Highland Park. My feeling was that there were still a few teachers there who were not giving students a chance, showing that they believed in them and providing that extra encouragement and help. (Often students don't take advantage of the counselor until they get a paper directing them to the counselor, and then it's usually too late.) If I could go there and improve the culture and be the strongest ally of the students, then I could make a difference and feel fulfilled.

They assigned me to Highland Park, and when I arrived, a few of the teachers who had not encouraged me asked me what I was doing there. I said that I was there to do *their* job. They were not happy about that. Fortunately many of the teachers had been helpful and continued to be supportive to the kids.

One of the recurring issues at any school is that many of the teachers and counselors focus on the high-achieving kids from wealthier families, while kids from poor families are given up for lost and don't receive that all-important push. It's a compliment to the school when kids get into a great college or university, and it also helps the school's ratings. But what about the others—the 25 percent who with encouragement and mentoring could also have a shot at a future?

There was some friction at Highland Park when I first arrived, as some teachers thought I was too "buddy buddy" with the kids. The students were coming to me for help because they trusted me. I would go through the College Possible program with the kids, and I was able to help a number of them get motivated to attend college.

Some students don't go to school because they just don't like school. Others have stuff going on at home that they won't discuss with teachers or counselors. Often counselors don't ask the kids pertinent questions but simply criticize them for not showing up. Open communication is often lacking.

I took a different approach, inviting kids in and getting them to tell me what was going on and why they weren't in class. Some had dysfunctional families at home, others had to take care of younger siblings, still others had to work nearly full time to keep the family going. What I did was simply listen, let them know I cared, and tell them a little about my own struggles. Only then would I begin to encourage them, help them resolve their problem, and get them back into class. The students would often prefer to come to me rather than respond to a letter from a counselor whom they felt would not understand their situation. Most of these were kids of color: Hispanic, Hmong, Asian, African, Native American, and African American. Many were recent immigrants who had issues with language and culture shock. They often felt like they were being targeted by the administration and relentlessly criticized.

After my two-year term of service at Americorp ended in June of 2013, I went to work for Wells Fargo, doing mortgage work for a short time in Eagan. While the pay was good and I had no problem doing the work, my heart was just not in that game; it was not the right fit for me. I gave them my notice, returned to my Highland Park neighborhood, and volunteered working with kids. One of the volunteer coordinators I met was in management at College Possible, and he suggested I apply again in case an opening came up. It did, and I submitted my resume one more time. Several weeks later I was accepted to the position of program coordinator for the mentoring program. My job is to recruit professional adults in the metropolitan area who are interested in making a difference in our young students' lives in terms of their writing skills and professionalism. We match adults in one-on-one relationships with students based on both personal and career interest. I was in New York recently, and they have a similar program called I Mentor that has matched professionals up with more than three thousand students.

College Possible's base program in the Twin Cities is in twenty high schools, and we have the mentoring program up and running in three. In our program we have an online platform where the mentor and volunteer can connect. Each week my colleagues and I come up with a topic for the student to write about. It could be about math or science or sports or the advantages of a college education. The pairs are required to meet once a month at an event hosted by College Possible. In terms of the total College Possible program, we're finding that students who have a mentor do better than those who don't. In my own case I never had a mentor. The notice was there, and a coach dealing with forty students came to the school, but the added push from a mentor was not there. I was lucky to be pretty much of a self-starter.

My older brother was into science and engineering. He attended the University of Minnesota and now works for Boeing. He just got his masters degree. My sisters both have families. My younger brother says he doesn't like school, so we're working on him.

My parents were always checking on us to make sure we did our homework. Although they had not gone to college, they totally supported our education and wanted us to go as far as we could with it.

Sometimes I'm asked if I would rather have gone to the University of Minnesota than Southwest University, where the racial bias was so bad I didn't want my parents to visit me there. My response to that question is absolutely not. I learned a lot from that experience and became a better person for it.

I enjoy my work very much. In terms of the future, I'm planning to get a masters from St. Thomas University in computer science. I'm pretty good with the new technology, and that should help with whatever the future has in store for me.

When I asked Cherkos about what might have happened to him without the introduction to College Possible, he told me that because of the influence his parents had on him, he feels he might still have been able to get into a community college later in life, though it might have taken him seven or eight more years because of added work required to pay the tuition himself. If he had gone to one of the other schools, he told me, he would have wound up with a huge load of college loan debt that would have limited his future options. It's interesting to speculate on the impact of College Possible and its mentoring program on kids from families without two caring parents or where there is abuse and neglect at home.

Beth Milbrandt

"My peers on the reservation would make fun of me, saying they could make more money selling drugs than I could working. They would sit around and watch TV and drive their four wheelers. While I should have known better, at the time the attraction of selling drugs was too high."

Beth had gotten off work early the day we met, which was a blessing for me since we had been trying to connect for some time. She told her story of struggling with the lack of opportunity, and the effect of peer pressure in her early days on the reservation, with a calmness that gave no indication of the life-threatening experience she'd had a few hours earlier. She clearly was at peace with herself and the world around her.

I was born in 1978 and grew up in Cass Lake, Minnesota, which is a high-poverty area with a lot of crime. It's on the reservation, where there is not a lot to do. I got involved in drinking and using drugs. There is not a lot of work up there—just a Walmart and Target in Bemidji—so it's pretty quiet.

My parents were both teachers. My dad was the athletic director at Cass Lake Schools and very involved in the community. My older brother passed away from cancer when he was twenty-seven.

I went to grade school and high school there and started selling drugs at an early age. That was my way of life and how I made money. Life on the reservation was depressing and my peers would make fun of me, saying they could make more money selling drugs than I could working. They would sit around and watch TV and drive their four wheelers. While I should have known better, at the time the appeal of selling drugs was too high. The process sort of escalates, as you try working but don't get ahead, and then see how easy the drug money can be. I started selling marijuana and then moved up to meth.

Drugs were cheaper in the Twin Cities so I moved there to live in 2000. In 2005 I got caught selling methamphetamines in north Minneapolis. That put me in federal prison in Texas for five years.

My time in prison in Texas did nothing to help me learn more about myself or to build new skills. It did, however, convince me that this was a place I never wanted to see ever again. I made some pretty good friends there, and we were able to share stories about mistakes we had made. This was a beginning for me in developing some new life skills. I had had a baby just before I went there, and of course I missed all of her early years.

After five years in Texas, I was sent to a new women's facility in Waseca, Minnesota. I enrolled in a federal drug rehab program there called the Residential Drug Abuse Program [RDAP] that helped me see the impact of my behavior on those around me, like my parents and daughters. They helped me see myself in a new way, and especially the pain I had brought to others. The program involves role playing and learning to better identify your feelings. Most of my friends who went through the

RDAP program have gotten good jobs and are OK now. Once I committed to changing my life, my parents stood behind me and helped with housing and taking care of the children. That program also helped me understand what I was doing and why I was doing it, and it taught me how to start a new life once I got out. They have little stepping stones of things you have to remember to lead a clean life. That was very helpful.

Eventually I was released to a halfway house and began my search for a job. As a felon it was very difficult to find a job. Even Walmart and Target, who are supposed to be felon friendly, were not receptive. After searching in the Twin Cities for seven months I went back to Cass Lake and sought work in Bemidji, where my daughter and parents lived. There was nothing available there for me. I really had lost all hope.

I had heard about Summit Academy OIC [Opportunity Industrialization Center] from a guy I was in the halfway house with who had studied carpentry. That was something I knew I wanted to do. So I went to Summit and told them that I had a poor work history and was a felon besides. They said, "Don't worry about it...we will help you."

I started at Summit in September of 2012. Without Summit I would probably still be on welfare, living in my parents' basement with little hope for my future.

Your first day at Summit is one of learning the rules and getting oriented to the classrooms. Then you pick your career track, and I picked carpentry as I had done some of that in prison in Texas. The classes run from 8:30 a.m. to 3:00 p.m.. Every race and ethnicity you can imagine was in my group. We all had different views on things. OSHA classes dealt with safety, and then there were all the technical courses related to carpentry, including learning about all the tools and the different materials. This involved a lot of math. We would build small houses and then take them apart. We worked as a team so we had to figure out how to decide things as a group. We also had classes on communication, which helped on the job as well as with my family. My tuition was covered by government support plus philanthropy.

Summit also has a "brown bag" program called Women Wear Hard Hats Too. All the groups of women who train here come for lunch and talk about issues related to women, such as how to handle inappropriate behavior by others and how to appropriately assert yourself on a work crew. Family issues are discussed, and it gives us a chance to share our problems and learn from one another. This program has been so well received that something comparable is starting with the men.

Summit helped me get a job with Braxton Hancock construction company, the largest construction framing company in Minnesota. I have learned a lot there and have joined the union.

They gave me medical insurance and a pension plan, which are things I never dreamed of having. Now I could afford a car that didn't break down all the time and have medical support for my kids. It's a great feeling to be able to put money away for my retirement. When I was laid off at Braxton between projects, I was picked up by Central Roofing Company. Right now I'm working on the Loring Tower that looks out over the park in downtown Minneapolis. We're doing the weather-proofing on the exterior deck walls. This building is going to be thirty-six stories tall, and today we were up on twenty-nine.

The Central Roofing job came about because I spoke at a Summit Academy OIC donor event. I explained to the group what my situation was, what I had been through, and told them I had felt pretty much hopeless but that Summit had saved my life. Warren Stock happened to be there and said, "Really? You're laid off right now? Come and see me tomorrow and we will get you started on the paperwork." That was my start with Central Roofing. You see, these construction companies are required to hire a certain percentage of women and minorities on major projects.

The OSHA training I received at Summit may have saved my life today. This morning I was working on the twenty-ninth floor of the Loring Tower, priming the walls before we put on the covering. I stepped around a corner on the concrete edge of the twenty-ninth floor and slipped on the ice. I was priming the outside wall with a roller and I had to reach back over the edge. Then I fell back over the side. Luckily my safety rope was tight and I was able to get back on. Because of the ice we got off early today.

One of the great things about Summit is that when you do something right you get a pat on the back like, "That's the way to go, Milbrandt." I never heard that before, and I can't tell you what a difference a compliment like that makes. Five days a week I am here working, and I'm with my kids in Bemidji on weekends. It works well. My kids brag about my work, telling their friends what I do up on these tall buildings. I feel good knowing they're proud of me. Now I can afford to take my kids to a Twins game. They want pictures of where I work so they can tell their friends. My parents dote on my kids, who are thirteen and eight.

Now I can begin to think about my future. I'm involved with the Carpenters and Joiners Union, Local 322. I would like to work my way up in the union some day. The first woman instructor at Summit Academy OIC was from Local 322. So who knows what the future might hold for me. Life is good now!

I asked Beth what recommendations she might make to elected officials and policy makers about rehabilitation programs for former offenders. She responded that there is tremendous pressure when one gets out of prison facilities to find housing and then get the training necessary for a living-wage job. If you have no family support, the dollars just aren't there. She feels that the support for residential halfway housing should be extended for a longer period of time than six months so one can stay settled during the time it takes to train for a job. Also, she feels a modest stipend for toiletry essentials would help with basics of grooming. Otherwise, she believes just trying to survive can bring people back to their former drug-dealing lifestyles since the money attraction is so great. She says just a modest amount of support upon release can reduce the recidivism rate and lower the cost to taxpayers.

One can't help but be inspired by Beth's story. Despite coming from a strong family, she slid into using and selling drugs due to boredom and peer pressure. Good recreational facilities and mentors at Cass Lake might have made a huge difference in her early years. She tells her story with a sense of quiet gratitude for the support she received from Summit Academy and employers willing to take a chance with her. Beth is proud of what she's accomplished and candid about recommendations to improve our rehabilitation programs.

Shegitu Kebede

"I had been raped three times in Ethiopia by soldiers and was pregnant. I had so much anger and hate inside of me. One night I got up, got on my knees, and said, "God, if you are real, take this hate out of me. I don't want to be angry anymore... I want to be joyful like the rest of them... so God, just let me know."

The Flamingo Restaurant is tucked down a quiet side street off University Avenue in St. Paul, Minnesota. East African cuisine, prepared by its remarkable owner, Shegitu Kebede, is its specialty. One feels a profound sense of hope for humanity as she tells her story of overcoming the most painful degradations that refugee women experience when war destroys the fabric of one's community. There is a beauty to this striking African woman that is both spiritual and physical. There is a calmness that suggests she has found peace with her creator. She has overcome the worst and is now experiencing the best, and her smile suggests deep gratitude for the guidance given to her by her many mentors.

I don't remember my parents as I was very young when placed in an orphanage run by missionaries in Ethiopia. The community surrounding the orphanage and boarding school was very supportive, and I had everything a child needs. I remember gardening, playing sports, knitting, drama, choir practice, and bible study. I didn't appreciate all of that until much later, when I was a teenager. When I was about ten the missionaries were forced to leave. The political climate was changing in the direction of communism, and missionaries were no longer welcome. What had been a loving community was taken away from me by the revolution. Now I was able to compare life before and after. So my life was shattered and I completely left God. The people who remained at the orphanage were not able to answer my many questions, and the nature of the religious teachings became less personal. The teachers didn't appear to be living the life they were teaching. My brothers and I were still required to go to church, but the meaning was gone. I just sat there—my mind was somewhere else.

By the time I arrived in Kenya at age seventeen I had made up my mind that I wanted nothing to do with God. I felt God was a hypocrite just like the people who had taken over the orphanage. I was placed along with three other girls in a temporary halfway home funded by a Catholic organization. The other girls were going to a non-denominational Christian church and invited me to join them. At first I refused, but they eventually wore me down. So once again I sat there with my mind somewhere else. One day I noticed a girl I had known at the boarding school in Ethiopia singing in the choir. She urged me to become more involved, but I would have nothing to do with it. However, over time I observed how joyful she was; she was no longer the person I had known before. Her love for God and love for people were real, though I said to myself, "Are you kidding me?" There were others like her who were not refugees who were reaching out to us.

Some of these people were very well to do and had nothing to gain by reaching out to us. Seeing that, I began to wonder if maybe there were two parts to this, and maybe this God was OK for me. By then I had also gone through so much personal pain. I had been raped three times in Ethiopia by soldiers and was pregnant. I had so much anger and hate inside of me. As a teenager I was not at peace with myself, and I wanted to know what made these others so calm and loving. One night I got up, got on my knees, and said, "God, if you are real, take this hate out of me. I don't want to be angry anymore. I want to be joyful like the rest of them...so God, just let me know."

That next morning I got up and felt I had become a peaceful person. I felt like something had just washed me clean. There was no residue left in me. That was the day I gave my life to God. Since then I have had a peace and joy that have never left me. I have had many ups and downs in my life, but the joy has stayed inside of me all the way. It wasn't the preacher of the church or even the teachings that turned me around. It was simply seeing their lives and how happy and loving they were. I wanted to be just like them. Since that day I have never felt the need to go to a counselor or therapist.

This, then, was my new life for three and a half years. I worked and went to school there, since you then have to wait a year after getting your United Nations formal identification as a refugee before you can ask for asylum. During that year the United Nations no longer supports you. I was fortunate to receive a scholarship to become a beautician and later worked in a beauty salon. After that I found work at a Christian radio station in Nairobi.

As a refugee you don't get to choose what country, state, or city you go to. I applied to the American, Canadian, and

Australian embassies. I was accepted by the American embassy, who then began the process of finding a sponsor for me. There is a not-for-profit organization that actually seeks out the sponsor, sets the timetable, works with the airlines, and follows through on the entire process.

At the time, I had been married for only three months to a man I met briefly before the war. One reason I married so young was to protect my brothers. The army would take young men from poor areas who had no family. I thought that if I married and settled down I could take care of them and save them from the war. Kids fourteen and up were randomly taken from the orphanage at that time. The people who ran the orphanage simply didn't care. Sadly, I lost one of my brothers in the war. There were wars with Eritrea, Somalia, and then the civil struggle within the country against the communists.

My journey took me from Nairobi to New York and then on to Fargo, North Dakota. I was met by a delegation from four churches who were working together to sponsor me. They were Catholic, Episcopalian, and Lutheran. It was November and cold and snowing. They brought us appropriate clothing. I never dreamed that people could live in that kind of cold. Nothing was green, there was only white everywhere. I thought this was the way it would be all year long. My son was three years old at the time.

Four women from the churches showed us to a furnished apartment and provided us with the food, clothing, and other essentials that we needed. Each had a different assignment, such as arranging for a medical check-up or helping us learn English, find a job, or get our children into preschool. Someone showed us how to use public transportation, another told us where to shop.

I found work as a nurse's aide and later in a factory doing electrical wiring. The people who helped me were the most amazing people I have ever met.

There was another African family there from Eritrea, and they welcomed us with an African meal. When I woke up the next morning, that was a shock. It had snowed. Everything was white! It was so depressing to think I was going to live in a country without grass or a garden or seeing a leaf or any green-ery. North Dakota is very flat, and as far as you could see it was all white.

I wrote back home to my friends telling them that it was not just the people that were white: everything, including the land, was white. It didn't occur to me that this might ever change. It was such a lonely feeling because I didn't know the language and couldn't ask questions or express my feelings in any way.

About three months after we arrived I was watching this movie on TV and I laughed for the first time since I arrived. It was hilarious, even though I didn't fully understand what was going on. I asked myself, Will I ever be able to laugh like that again? At the time you think you will never overcome such difficulties.

My work went well and the people were very accepting of me. Eventually another refugee Ethiopian family came from Somalia, and by that time I knew enough English to be the translator for their sponsor. That family moved in next to me with their little daughter, so the kids played and we became close friends. That family had friends who had come over and settled in Minneapolis, and when they decided to join them I wanted to go along. The Ethiopian Christian Fellowship on Franklin Avenue near Augsburg College welcomed us, so now we were Minnesotans.

After we settled in my husband arrived from Ethiopia, and that's when the domestic abuse started. My husband was the breadwinner at the time. I had not had parents so I wanted very much to have a family and raise my children. I worked very hard to please my husband, trying this and that and everything they say you are supposed to do. My thinking was that maybe if I cooked better or became a better housekeeper or whatever, things might work out. That was not the case, so after thirteen years of marriage we divorced in 2003. At the time I was a nurse's aide at Fairview University Hospital and later worked at Common Bond, the non-profit affordable housing provider, as a social worker. I was living in the neighborhood and volunteered there; they liked what I did and decided to hire me part-time.

After that I started my cleaning business. Many refugees came through my office at Common Bond, and while many of the men found work, for the women it was a different story. They didn't have the appropriate education or work experience so I decided to help them out. Along with training them in the cleaning business, we started to teach English as a second language, citizenship training, cooking and sewing, and all the other things new immigrants need to learn. These women were then able to find work at different places like Augsburg College and Fairview Hospital. I have been doing that now for about six years. Through my volunteer work on boards dealing with affordable housing and other issues confronting new immigrants, I have been able to make valuable connections in the Twin Cities community.

Joe Errigo was executive director of Common Bond at the time, and he was kind enough to write letters to a number of organizations and building owners saying that I was well qualified, had been their employee for many years, and could be trusted to do excellent work. That was so helpful. And in turn, after we would sign on to new cleaning clients, we would ask them to recommend us to their friends if they liked our work. That was also helpful. In the first year of my business, I was able to get thirty-eight women trained and hired. Some of these people couldn't read at the time so we taught them to recognize various cleaning materials by sight, touch, and smell. They were also taught the different requirements for cleaning in hospitals and in people's homes.

One of my worries was about the small children of these African immigrants. I didn't want my children or theirs sitting at home watching TV all day while their moms were at work. Most of the women came from very low income households, and many lived in high-rise public housing. So I started an after-school program, recruiting students from the University of Minnesota, Augsburg College, and Minneapolis Community and Technical College to sit with the children one-on-one and teach them how to read and write.

Many of the moms were getting phone calls every day from school saying that their kids had been acting up. I didn't understand this and wondered why was this happening. So, after getting permission from the parents, I visited the school. The problem was not with the students' learning ability. It turned out that these refugee kids were being put into classes according to their age, regardless of their language skills or level of general educational. Eighth-grade kids didn't want their peers to know they didn't know how to read, so they would create a fuss in class and the teacher would excuse them.

There was a small room in my office that we set up as a tutoring room for kids who didn't know how to read and write. Volunteers worked with the kids even if they had to start with the ABCs. I paid for the space and materials by putting aside 25 percent of the money I made from my cleaning business. The Minneapolis newspaper wrote about my training program, which inspired the McKnight Foundation to grant me an award. So news of my work was getting out, and that's how I met influential people—like Joe Selvaggio, who I met through a friend of mine who worked at a non-profit called Books for Africa. That was in 2006. Joe became my mentor. He wanted to make sure that I took care of myself and sometimes helped me with money. When I spent it on shoes for the kids he would scold me, saying, "That was for you!" He helped me structure my business more effectively using modern management tools.

Others who were helpful included Hussein Samatar, who headed the African Development Center and served on the Minneapolis School Board. I met him while serving on an advisory committee for the Payne Avenue and Lake Street neighborhoods when Lake Street was under construction. Also, I took classes from Mike Temali of the Neighborhood Development Center [NDC] and then started a business class for immigrant women who had their own little shops. Hussein was very helpful to me in training these women to develop sound financial practices. One of my concerns was that these women have access to safe, affordable housing, so we partnered with NDC through their home ownership class to help some of them buy their first home.

Going Home was the name of my cleaning business. My goal was to help these women earn enough to move beyond simply getting through the day. If they could earn a living wage and find decent housing, then they could become valuable citizens and in turn make their own contribution to the community. It was important to partner with established organizations like the

University of Minnesota and Augsburg College so that when my people performed well they would get the benefits, and they would be less likely to be laid off when budgets were trimmed. Barb Janetta of Local Initiative Support Corporation [LISC] was helpful to me at that time. LISC conducted classes in leadership at Metropolitan State University. I also met Hussein Samatar there. Barb Janetta was my guide in working through many of the challenges that confronted me in developing Going Home.

Mike Temali and the Neighborhood Development Center were also a great help when I started my restaurant. They helped us develop our business plan, logo, "Flamingo" name, menu, accounting systems, and marketing program. We started the business in 2010, just when the Central Corridor light rail construction started between Minneapolis and St. Paul. With all the traffic issues involved, we simply couldn't have launched the business without NDC. The earlier work I had done on the advisory committee when Lake Street was under construction was very helpful in surviving the tear-up on University Avenue.

In 2008 I was invited by a group of women from Stillwater to be the keynote speaker at a national Presbyterian women's conference. Anne Rock from that church, along with some other women, decided after my speech they wanted to adopt me as one of their own. So this was another group that gave me moral support.

We started the restaurant in 2010. One year earlier we had looked at the building, for which the owner wanted $75,000. We were part of a group that offered $65,000. That offer was not accepted so we continued with our cleaning business and community work. One year later, just before Christmas, the owner called my partner at about 3:00 a.m. and said, "I don't know why but I'm going to sell the restaurant to you and your partner and not those other people." My partner said, "But we don't have the money!" He said that that was alright. We could pay him off as we went along. We couldn't believe it! That's just how God worked it out for us.

We had no idea that the streets were going to be torn up at the time.

So many people have been helpful to me over the years after I share my story. My volunteer work put me in contact with so many good people who were willing to listen and then be helpful. People like Suzanne Kochevar, Randy Morrison, Joe Selvaggio, and so many others picked me up when my spirits were down because of abuse, divorce, or some other problem. They helped me to visualize a promising future. What I have been given by these people is a million times what I have returned to the community. They are the kind of people who would come in a minute if I cried out for help.

We have a bunch of women who get together every month to cook and visit. We put money aside for the group, and if someone has a special need, like a car or education or training for a job or the down payment for a home, we help out. That's how many of us as immigrants get started because we don't have a credit rating and the banks are not interested in us.

My youngest child is in her third year at Biola University in California. My son, who is the oldest, lives here and has a baby so now I am a grandmother. With respect to my future, I want to start a school in a refugee camp in Ethiopia. I have raised about 75 percent of the money already. It will be open to all refugees from Africa to help them learn other languages and prepare them for the immigration process.

As I mentioned earlier, due to U.S. financial constraints you are allowed only ninety days to learn the required skills once you arrive in the United States. That is not enough time! That is why I want to teach them in camps *before* they come. Trying to teach them fast and cram everything in once they arrive isn't the right way to help them become productive citizens. We should want them to have all the skills they need to survive so they can become productive members of whichever society they choose to live in much sooner.

This remarkable woman has opened my eyes to what the United States should have been undertaking to a much greater extent these past several decades. New immigrants from Europe, Asia, Central and South America, and Africa have reinvigorated our economy over the years in both urban centers and rural communities. With most economists predicting a shortage of skilled and semi-skilled workers over the next several decades, it is essential that our immigration process do what it can to attract the best and the brightest from abroad. This will require new investment in recruitment and training well before individuals reach our shores.

Raymond Jackson

"For people like me who have post-traumatic stress disorder, Ujamaa Place is the place to be because it can save your life. It has become the home I never had."

Ujamaa Place reminds us that there is a lost generation of young African American men in our community. These men have lived many years in poverty, without strong male role models; they have limited education, little or no real job experience, often have been involved in gang activity and spent time in jail. Without effective intervention they will likely spend most of their life in jail or be dead by the time they are thirty-five.

My name is Raymond Jackson. I am from St. Paul, Minnesota. I'm thirty-three years old, certified with post-traumatic stress disorder, and receive social security disability income. I have had a lot of trauma in my life. Child abuse was a huge issue for me, and I'd like to describe a few things related to that that contributed to my downfall. Then, I want to share with you how I got back on my feet and enjoyed some success.

As far as I can remember—and this goes back to when I was five years old—my mother took me, my cousin, my sister, and my big brother Durrell next door to a neighbor's house. She didn't know them. She knocked on the door, faked an emergency, and left us there. She said she would be right back. This Latino family agreed to keep us for an hour, but my mother didn't return for many months. The police finally located her. That was my first memory of what I later came to understand as abuse and neglect.

After that, times got really bad for me. I knew there was some sort of love in my mother's heart because she loved everybody else dearly, but she treated me very roughly. I believe this was because my dad used to abuse her, and I looked just like him. He used to tie her hands to the bed and shave her hair off. He once kicked her teeth out, and to this day she has only two teeth in her mouth. After enduring all that pain from him, she started in on me. When I was eight, a game of follow-the-leader took hold of my family. After my mom tortured me, my older brother and cousin would come after me. Once they took me to the basement and wrapped me up with Saran Wrap like a mummy to the point where my arm broke. They turned the lights off and I was scared out of my wits, crying and getting sick on myself. I don't remember much but I do remember my mother coming down and beating me. Maybe she thought I couldn't feel the pain.

As I listened to Raymond I was struck by his humility and sense of gratitude for what has become a new life for him. He speaks softly, without anger, as he describes the painful abuse by his mother and others. He understands the cycle of abuse that passes from generation to generation and sees himself as one stop on that circular pathway of destructive behavior.

Of course I was afraid to tell anybody about any of that, and as I grew up I just stuffed it all inside. But it put me in the hospital mental ward four times, and I even tried suicide. The damage was pretty serious. I later joined a gang—the Rolling Sixties Crips. With gang life things went from bad to worse for me. I was in jail at twenty-three and later made my fifth suicide attempt. But just when I had completely given up hope, I heard a little voice as I was asking for help. I don't know if it was God or not because I didn't believe in God. In fact, through all that time I was cursing God. But I heard a voice, and I said, "I give up, and if you can just help me I will try to help someone else." I was trying to believe. Then lots of good things started happening for me.

For one thing, through some friends I heard about Ujamaa Place.

Young men who come to organizations like Ujamaa Place for the most part grew up without a father or positive male role model, feel lonely and unloved, lack an understanding of being responsible for their actions, generally have low self-esteem, are unable to develop lasting relationships, are quick to anger, and identify themselves as being part of an unwanted subculture. They are unable to visualize a future, lack basic academic skills, are accustomed to failure, more often than not are homeless, have dropped out of school, and usually lack employable skills.

I was in the process of getting my GED at the Hubbs Center school and I needed to pass the math test. My friend said there was this math wizard at Ujamaa Place who could help me. He kept after me every day and finally I decided to contact them. I knew I needed help in math to get my GED. My goal was to get that help and then leave. I met the math wizard—his name was Kadar—and my math scores improved. He told me to hang around a bit, get to know everyone, and see how I liked the place. I soon discovered math isn't the only thing they can help you with. I heard about their empowerment program and how they groom young African American men to get some direction in life and become better role models for their children. I really enjoyed that because I had never had that kind of love before. It was the first time that I ever felt loved and appreciated.

For people like me who have post-traumatic stress disorder, this is the place to be because Ujamaa can save your life. I have been homeless for sixteen years. They gave me housing. I have gone from zero to sky high. Ujamaa place has become the home I never had. Now I see what love is all about. When I was going through my difficult years I never had any real friends. My best friend now is a character I have developed through my artwork. I've written a kid's book called *Biblett the Frog*. I know it sounds crazy, but Bibett is my only true friend. I took my artwork and story line to Kinko's and got a rough copy of the book printed. I love drawing with ink pens and color pencils.

Raymond led me through the book, which takes imaginary animals who are friends down a series of candy roads where they encounter some frightening monsters and serious challenges. The final episode involves saving a friend from captivity at the temple of doom. Raymond lent me the book with the admonition to not bend the corners and handle it carefully. It's well written, and my wife, Anne, (an accomplished artist herself) describes the artwork as extraordinary. Is this book something more than just a story about fictitious characters? It most likely is.

I have always been multi-talented. I can write poetry, speak at motivational events, and cook like you wouldn't believe. Maybe I can grow my love for cooking into a business. Tyler Perry from Meaia's play *Family Reunion* reminds me that if I could just focus on one thing and stick to it, I could really make something of myself. You see, I have a problem juggling all this stuff around and trying to stay focused on one thing.

Most of the men here at Ujamaa Place come because of a court order, though others just heard about it and showed up. I hear them talking about this place at the bus stop. I feel pretty safe here. Some folks here know that there are people out there who would like to harm them. Many of us just come here to volunteer and help out. We feel protected here. I walked through the fire in my former life and now I'm on the mountain top. Whatever they want me to do I will do. I love to speak to groups about this place, what happened to me, and how Ujamaa Place helped me. Once I get back on my feet, make some money, and feel secure, I'm going to tell it all. There is a lot of bad stuff going on out there, and the people in power need to hear about it. I hope I can help some people avoid the kind of abuse that I suffered when I was growing up.

One of these days I want to make a movie about my story. I will have to change my name to be safe, but I will tell my story for sure. What they did to me was cruel. It was evil.

Raymond showed me a variety of mug shots he carries on his iPhone. As he mentioned, he has been in jail twenty-three times. In these photos you can see the struggle he has had. He has a lot of talent, and with continued help from Ujamaa and others he can make it. Ujamaa Place itself is simply a series of small meeting rooms on the second floor

of an older building in the Midway District of St. Paul, Minnesota. Their comprehensive approach offers young men a route to success through intensive counseling and training in six areas: empowerment skills, completing their GED, job search and job skills, spirituality, African American culture, and life skills.

One can only speculate about where the cycle of abuse started that caused Raymond's father to abuse his mother. In any case, the pattern that followed damaged many lives and impacted the surrounding community. It is a hopeful sign that Ujamaa Place, which began in 2011 and served 154 men that year, has had a 40 percent rate of continued participation, in contrast to a typical continuance rate of 20 to 25 percent in other rehabilitation programs. Of the thirty who had been in prison, none have re-offended! The national Institute for Justice reports that children who are abused or neglected are 53 percent more likely to be arrested as a juvenile and 38 percent more likely to be arrested as an adult. When abuse and neglect are reported and followed up with publicly-financed home visitation by a public health nurse, family behavior improves dramatically, which results not only in healthier families but also in considerable long-term savings to taxpayers. But abuse is often not reported, as was the case with Raymond. As well-structured pre-kindergarten centers become more prevalent, the ability to identify and report abuse should improve. Perhaps as relevant as all the specialized training that occurs at Ujamaa Place is Raymond's comment at age thirty-three, "It was the first time I felt loved and appreciated."

Ibro Tabakovic

"In the middle of October 1992 my Serbian friend, who was an officer in the Serbian army, came to my house late in the night to tell me that my life is in danger and recommended that I leave the town immediately."

"We were traveling from Banja Luka to Belgrade through the famous Serbian "corridor," passing by destroyed and empty villages and cities with a lot of abandoned domestic animals, but without people."

Science has an extraordinary ability to jump international borders and, through publications and conferences, connect many of the world's best and brightest thinkers. In this remarkable story, such global connections saved a family's life, brought new scientific expertise to the United States, advanced the product capabilities of one of our leading high-tech companies, and created some remarkable new friendships. I had the privilege of meeting Ibro and Katmerka Tabakovic at a holiday party shortly after they came to Minnesota. Their story of surviving the ethnic cleansing following the breakup of the former Yugoslavia involved numerous friends who honored their many contributions to their community and country.

I came to the United States on March 1, 1993, as a refugee, accompanied by my wife, Katmerka, and our sons, Muhamed and Mirza. We were forced to leave our home in the city of Banja Luka against our will, due to the widespread so-called "ethnic cleansing" that took place in the Bosnian war from 1992 to 1995.

My life as a child had been pretty happy. My grade school was in a very fine school in Banja Luka and I later went to university in Zagreb. I majored in chemical engineering and got my PhD in organic chemistry. I was asked to assist with graduate students and then was elected to the position of docent, which is like an associate professor, and then became an assistant professor. I was about twenty-one when I first met my wife, Katmerka, who was five years younger than me. She would also work to get her PhD in chemistry. We married when we were studying at the university in Zagreb. So, looking back, between the two of us we have five advanced degrees and two children!

One of my friends was the mayor of Banja Luka, and they were opening a new university there. He invited us to be part of that. It was a huge opportunity to be part of a new venture in your hometown. I was doing post-graduate study in Southhampton, England, at the time, which was the academic center for electrical engineering. While leaving a huge cultural and academic center like Southhampton was difficult, the idea of being part of something new in my hometown was compelling. We moved. I became professor, full professor, vice president, and eventually president of the University of Banja Luka, all within the space of four years between 1981 and 1985. I worked hard to make the university well known, especially in the fields of organic and electrical chemistry. That is how I met my American friend Professor Larry Miller, who taught at the University of

Minnesota. We met at a conference in Germany where we were both presenting research papers. I visited him at the University of Minnesota in 1980, and seven years later he came to Banja Luka. At that time we were working together on a joint USA/ Yugoslav project. I considered him to be the best in the field we were working in. We were both professional colleagues and personal friends.

There is an old Latin saying: *Historia est magistra vitae*. History is the teacher of life. To understand the recent upheavals in the Balkans, I need to say a few words about the history of Bosnia. It was originally on the border between the eastern and western Roman Empire. From the ninth to the eleventh century Bosnia was a Christian country. The Bosnian church was more Protestant than Catholic or Orthodox. Women were allowed to be priests, and the church was also a primary school as well as a place for learning the trades. The western Roman Empire included Slovenia and Croatia, which were Catholic. When the Turks occupied Bosnia, they said Bosnia could rule itself if it converted to Islam, so the Bosnians did so. The point is that going way back in its history, Bosnia has always been fiercely independent from neighboring political and religious influences.

Although over time our people were Catholic, Orthodox, Muslim, and Protestant, we were united as Bosnians. During the Second World War we fought together against fascism. The Germans were in Belgrade from 1941 to 1945. They were also in Croatia. The partisans were able to slow down a number of German divisions during the war. Six of the seven German offenses against Tito were in our homeland of Bosnia. At that time I had no idea what religion any of my friends identified with. I never even thought about that. Roughly 30 percent of our people married across religious lines. Once, after we moved to the United

States, a nurse at the hospital asked me if I was Catholic, Jewish, or Muslim. I answered her that I was all of them!

The disintegration of Yugoslavia took place from 1987 to June 1990, when Slobodan Milosevic, president of Serbia, led a coup d'etat and became de facto commander of the Yugoslav National Army (JNA). He decided to forcibly expel Slovenia and Croatia from Yugoslavia and "amputate" the parts of Croatia inhibited by Serbs. National socialism grew in Serbia under Milosevic, and also in Croatia under former general of JNA Franjo Tudjman. Both of these nationalistic movements were in large part inspired by the same ideology as that of the fascistic armies defeated during the Second World War, of the Ustashas (in Croatia) and the Chetniks (in Serbia). In their propaganda, Milosevic and Tudjman applied almost all general properties of fascist ideology defined by Umberto Eco in his essay "Eternal Fascism"—fear of difference, xenophobia, selective populism, the cult of tradition, construing pacifism as tracking with the enemy, labeling disagreement as treason, and so on. Milosevic's regime and JNA attacked Croatia in 1991 in a war that ended just before the start of the Serbian conquest of Bosnia-Herzegovina in April 1, 1992, which had by that time been recognized by the UN as a sovereign and independent state. The war in Bosnia, with atrocities hitherto unseen in post-war Europe, was characterized by genocide of Bosnian Muslims, shelling of Sarajevo, rapes, concentration camps, and ethnic cleansing.

By August 1992 the ethnic cleansing was already over in the cities close to Banja Luka (Bosanski Novi, Prijedor, Bosanska Gradiska, Kozarac, Sanski Most, Celinac, Kotor Varos). In September most of the Bosnians (Muslims) and the Croats (Catholics) in Banja Luka—two thirds of the city population—were dismissed from their jobs by the Serbs (Orthodox Christians).

About ninety private firms were destroyed by explosives during the night, several people were killed, and political leaders were put in prison or concentration camps outside the city. A curfew was imposed for Bosnians and Croats from five at night to seven the next morning. I could identify, in one thought experiment, my feelings from that period in Banja Luka with feelings of the Jews in Nazi-Germany during 1938–1940. This was the beginning of the total ethnic cleansing.

One day in September 1992 Mr. Predrag Radic, the mayor of Banja Luka (and a university professor who become an influential Serbian nationalist, called me into my laboratory to tell me I was to meet with Mr. Cyrus Vance of the United States tomorrow at 5:00 p.m. at the Hotel Bosna in Banja Luka. I was very surprised by this invitation, but he explained to me that Mr. Cyrus Vance called him from his office in Zagreb (Croatia) to insist that he would like to talk personally with Professor Ibro Tabakovic (former president of the University of Banja Luka). Mr. Radic sounded very friendly, almost as he had a few years earlier when we used to meet at university meetings.

The next day I arrived on time at the Hotel Bosna. I knew that Mr. Cyrus Vance and Lord David Owen of England were coming to prevent the further ethnic cleansing of Bosnians and Croats from Banja Luka, since the ethnic cleansing in the cities around Banja Luka was already finished. I remember that Serbian leader Radovan Karadzic made the public statement that non-Serbs (Muslims, Croats, Jews, and others) could feel free and would not suffer any kind of discrimination. It very soon became obvious that Dr. Karadzic had lied again, but in those days people in Banja Luka still had the feeling and hope that the international community would not allow fascism to dominate the region.

At the Hotel Bosna, Mr. Cyrus Vance and Lord David Owen had meetings with the highest Serbian officials, led by Dr. Karadzic and with delegations from the political parties: SDS-Serbian party, HDZ-Croation party, and SDA-Muslim party. They met also with religious leaders from Muslim, Catholic, and Orthodox churches.

I met for roughly thirty minutes in a room with Mr. Cyrus Vance, Lord David Owen, and two other English-speaking individuals. I realized later that I was the only person who talked to them without an interpreter. It was clear that both gentlemen were exhausted already, and the meeting started very informally. I asked them what they would like me to talk about, and Mr. Cyrus Vance asked me the simple question: "How do you feel?" I answered by telling a joke: One Bosnian was falling from a window on the nineteenth floor, and another was standing by a window on the ninth floor. As the falling Bosnian was passing, the man on the ninth floor asked him: "How do you feel?" The falling Bosnian answered: "Don't worry, so far so good."

They realized that I felt like the falling Bosnian did, and they laughed. I knew they had already been informed about the real situation in Banja Luka during previous meetings with the representatives of HDZ and SDA parties, as well as by the Catholic and Muslim religious leaders, so I decided to talk about the situation at the University of Banja Luka.

I told them that many people (Muslims and Croats) had already been dismissed from their jobs. The most common reason for such action was that the male person or his son(s) had not enlisted in the Serbian army, or that a female employee's husband or son(s) had not enlisted. Some of the dismissals occurred without any kind of explanation, or only "this is a war." As a rule, the dean of the faculty, who signed the relevant document, was not allowed to give a copy of his decision to the dismissed person. We were not allowed to use the Latin alphabet in our lectures or official communications, but only the Cyrillic alphabet. This was a typical primitive expression of the Serbian "cult of tradition" at that time. They used simple formulas: the Latin = Catholic, Catholic = Croats, Catholic + Muslims = enemies. The students (mainly Croats and Muslims) who refused to go into the Serbian army were expelled from the school without being given the opportunity to transfer their records and documents elsewhere. A PhD student of mine, Emir Gunic, finished his PhD thesis but was not allowed to make a final defense of it because he was a Muslim. Mr. Cyrus Vance and Lord David Oven listening attentively without comments as I related this information. At the end of the meeting they wished me good luck and expressed their appreciation for the information about the situation at the University of Banja Luka.

The short public statement made by Mr. Cyrus Vance at the end of his visit to Banja Luka was in complete disagreement with the statement Dr. Radovan Karadzic had issued on the morning of the same day. About a week after their visit, my student Eduard Kuljanac came to my house to worn me that a group of drunken soldiers in a nearby bar had been talking about Vance and Owen's visit and mentioned my name with a great animosity, though none of the men knew me personally. Evidently I was one of the people accused by some Serbs of giving Mr. Vance a negative impression of the situation regarding ethnic cleansing.

In the middle of October 1992 my Serbian friend, who was an officer in the Serbian army, came to my house late at night to tell me that my life was in danger and recommended that I leave the town immediately. I took his advice and called my colleague in Belgrade, Professor Aleksandar Despic, who was the vice president of the Serbian Academy of Sciences and Art. More to the point, his colleague at the academy, Dobrica Cosic, was at that time serving as president of Milosevic's Yugoslavia. I talked to Cosic by phone, telling him that my life was in danger and explaining my situation. He reacted as a real friend and promised me that he would arrange for my wife and me to come and work on "official business" in Belgrade. At the time I was working on an interesting project—"Electrochemical Synthesis of Antitumor Vinblastine Alkaloids"—and I had already published the preliminary results in an international journal. He proposed that I should resume my research in Belgrade as a joint project of the University of Banja Luka and the Serbian Academy of Science and Arts. He contacted the local Serbian authorities in Banja Luka, pointed out the importance of the project for Serbia and Yugoslavia, and told them that I would be able to make the antitumor alkaloids, whose price on the market was twenty million dollars per kilogram, during my scheduled three-month stay in Belgrade on "official business." This was highly exaggerated, since my work was in the early stages of the research, but the authorities in Banja Luka accepted the arguments.

In the afternoon of November 14, 1992, we got the message that the president of Yugoslavia, Dobrica Cosic, had provided safe transportation for us accompanied by all the required papers. His order was for two uniformed Serbian policemen (driver and officer) to bring us safely to Belgrade. The travel was scheduled for the next day, November 15, 1992, at 7:00 a.m. My younger son, Mirza, my wife, Katmerka, and I were packing the necessary things—one suitcase each—with a deep feeling of sorrow because we were leaving our native town, our family house, all our belongings, and our friends forever. I knew that it was going to be a one-way trip. We were relieved by the fact that our older son, Muhamed, had escaped from Banja Luka to Belgrade two months earlier.

We traveled from Banja Luka to Belgrade through the famous "Serbian corridor," passing by destroyed and empty villages and cities with a lot of abandoned domestic animals, but without people. The ethnic cleansing in Bosanski, Brod, Derventa, Prnjavor, Modrica, Odzak, Brcko, and Bijeljina was over. Disastrous pictures seen before only in horror movies had become our reality. During our voyage we were checked several times by the military and para-military police, but papers signed by Cosic and the policemen who accompanied us did the job. After twelve hours of traveling we arrived happily at the house of my mother-in-law, Naima Gluhbegovic, in Belgrade; she had been living in Belgrade for almost thirty years.

We stayed in Belgrade from November 15, 1992, to February 28, 1993. My wife and I were working at the Faculty of Science in the Institute of Organic Chemistry, on the Vinblastine project. In the meantime, we received news that we had been dismissed from our jobs in Banja Luka. The motive for our dismissal was that our son Muhamed did not respond to the invitation to join the Serbian army. The second piece of bad news we received was that two Serbian families had moved into our house and all the property inside it had been confiscated with permission of the local Serbian authorities in Banja Luka. The situation in Belgrade was much better than in Banja Luka, which was later described by UN officials as "a site of some of the war's worst human rights violation." Many of our Serbian colleagues in Belgrade were shocked by the destruction of cities like Sarajevo, Mostar, and others, and by atrocities on civilian population in Bosnia. They gave us moral support, which we needed so much during that time, and we will be thankful to them forever.

In about two month's time my family and I became homeless, jobless, and moneyless, so I decided to start looking for a new life abroad. I called my colleagues and friends, Professors L. L. Miller in the United States, H. Schafer in Germany, and H. Lund in Denmark, explaining my situation to them and asking for a temporary job. All three professors replied positively in January 1993. We decided to go to the United States and start our American dream. Professor Larry L. Miller from the University of Minnesota sent me an official invitation and all the necessary papers to come to the university's Department of Chemistry as a visiting professor.

As I look back on the period of the last twenty-one years of our lives in Minnesota, I can feel happy. This is the longest time our family has lived in one place, and it's been distinctively different from our life in Yugoslavia. The first few years are generally difficult for refugees who, according to my experience, are carrying two opposing psychological states, depression and positive energy to survive in a new world. I think that with the help of our new American friends we have succeeded in minimizing our depressive feelings while becoming self-supporting and productive. I worked at the University of Minnesota as a visiting professor for four years, teaching organic chemistry and working on research in the field of organic materials chemistry. I spent the next fifteen years at Seagate Technology working on research and development of the electrodeposition of magnetic materials for recording heads. For my work I have obtained several awards, of which the most important are from the Electrochemical Society in 2007 for outstanding research contributions in the field of electrodeposition, and entry into the Hall of Fame of Seagate Technology in recognition for published patents and innovations.

Through my friends I have begun to grasp the meaning of the American melting pot, and I've started considering Minnesota as my new homeland. The first of my American friends was Professor Larry Miller, as I mentioned earlier. We met at the Schools Elmau (Germany) Meeting on Organic Electrochemistry in June 1974. At that time Larry was in his early thirties and was a rising star in the relatively new field of organic electrochemistry—a hybrid of electrochemistry and organic chemistry. He published his results in the best scientific journals, and very often he was able to visualize new directions in this field. Hundreds of scientists around the world, including myself, were inspired by Larry's work. We met later on at scientific meetings in Scotland (1977), Denmark (1978), and the United States (1980). We cooperated on Joint Yugoslav/USA projects financed by National Science Foundation, which enabled me to visit Larry's laboratory at the University of Minnesota. Larry also visited me for a few days in 1987 at the University of Banja Luka. In the course of these professional meetings we became personal friends. I was much encouraged morally when, in June 1992, amid the Bosnian war, I received a fax from Larry. I don't remember the text exactly, but the message was on the order of: "Hang on, we're thinking about you!"

Larry introduced us to his friends, and we were very fortunate to be accepted as their friends too. People like Larry and his wife, Bobbie, Sonia and John Cairns, Shelly and John Brandl, Rita and Manny Kaplan, Libby and Dick Siegal, Suzan and Jack Flegler, Sheila and Phil Fishmann, Essie Kariv, and many others made us feel welcome. We shared many happy and sad moments in our lives during the last two decades.

This story has both a moral and an economic theme. Clearly the injustice suffered by Ibro and his family deserve the very best that America has to offer. This is what this country has stood for for centuries. Can any one of us imagine what it's like to lose overnight being president of a distinguished university and then having to abandon home and country and run for your life? When you sit with Ibro and hear him talk of his past, he is so at peace with himself and the world that you'd think he was describing someone else. Like so many before him, he has brought to our country technological expertise that has enriched our economy while at the same time giving new meaning and satisfaction to his life. As we often say, "God Bless America!"

Lante Morris

"You make good money selling crack, well over $1,000 per week. When you get involved in the drug trade nobody ever tells you about the risk. It's all about the money."

If it hadn't been for a perceptive parole agent, prison ministry program, and The NetWork for Better Futures, Lante Morris would likely still be in prison or at best unemployed. This is a remarkable story of failure and recovery that makes me proud to have met this inspiring young man.

For me life was pretty normal in the early days growing up as an urban kid. We had a home and all the essentials a kid needs. I was born in Gary, Indiana, and left there at age five for Milwaukee, where we lived for six years. Then my mom met a new boyfriend who told her about Minnesota, and things got rough. She got us settled in the Twin Cities when I was eleven. There were five of us children—three boys and two girls. My mom gave us the basics of a home, food on the table, and clothes on our back.

When I was about thirteen she started messing with drugs. That's when things started going downhill. My older brother and older sister wound up moving out because of my mom's

118

drug abuse. Me, my younger brother, and younger sister stayed at home with my mom. That's when I took on the role of making sure my older siblings helped pay the rent and I wound up acting like the father figure. That's when I learned to cook, which I love and am really good at.

My mother's drug problem took a toll on us, and that's when I stepped up and started selling candy at a youth club run by Jessie Anderson and Marion Etzwiler. That's where I learned about fast money; even though it was earned money it was fast money. It allowed me to help my brother and sister as well as my mom when she struggled with things. About a year later, when I was fourteen, I started selling drugs. My role models were some family members who were already into the game of selling drugs. I stayed in school for a while but dropped out when I was sixteen. In fact, I got kicked out because of a bad fight that broke out at Franklin Middle School in Minneapolis. From January until about May of that year, I pretended I was going to school but skipped that whole scene. I fooled around downtown with other kids and played basketball and football.

When you sell drugs, you buy them on the street or do a pay-back if someone gives them to you. You can always come out ahead if you do it right and avoid using your own product. I started with marijuana, and when I was eighteen got introduced to selling crack cocaine. I never used it but just sold it, though I did start smoking weed when I was nineteen. Other than weed the only drugs I ever did were Ecstasy and what some call PCP, or a form of it that's more like embalming fluid. You dip tobacco into it and smoke it, and it's definitely not good for you.

Crack is easier to conceal than marijuana. That was my business for the next ten years! In the process, I had two kids who are now really my world. My daughter, who is now ten, was born when I was twenty-two, and my son the next year. During that period I would work the street, then at night smoke and drink with friends, pass out, wake up, and then do it all over again. I would check on my little brother and sister from time to time and get some money to my mom when she needed it. You make good money selling crack, well over $1,000 per week. When you get involved in the drug trade nobody ever tells you about the risk. It's all about the money.

There are some really bad people out there, and then there is the question of the police. I wish I had been told about the risks involved, but nobody did that. It was all about the money and not the risk. I would have been better off selling candy. With candy there are no consequences unless someone tries to rob you or something like that. It's better to do things legally. I'm not mad at anyone about the journey I took because it's helped me be a better person today.

My dad was never around as he got locked up when I was eleven, which was about two months before we left Wisconsin. My aunt had moved to Minneapolis, and she told my mom to come here. More of my extended family moved up after the economy in Gary got bad.

There is no family history going back further than that.

During my ten years selling crack I wound up catching five felonies, two drug cases, one assault case, and a death from a person in a robbery. Prior to age twenty-nine the most time I did in a correctional institution was six months. Most of the time I did was in the county work house. There is no real program there— you just do your time. I had gotten my GED the year before, so I had made some progress on my education. I have been on parole ever since I caught my first offense at age eighteen. Every time I was about to get off, I would get caught for something else.

A number of different parole agents have been assigned to my case. Megan Daly is one who began to change my life for the better. She was helpful because she got me to focus on the future and remind me of my responsibility to my kids. She was patient when I slipped up, complimented me when I found work, and I really felt that she was in my corner.

That was all before my last situation, which was a robbery case. I was riding around with some friends, not really thinking about what we were doing, and we got out and jumped on someone. We knew we were committing a crime, but we had no idea it would turn into such a big deal. I ended up taking the time, and the other two people got away. The code on the street then was that you do not tell on your buddies even if they were the ones mainly responsible for the bad deed. They're now in prison and I'm free so it's amazing how God works sometimes. The guy said he remembered my jacket so that was it. I wound up doing thirteen months in St. Cloud and another thirteen in Fairbault, followed by eighty-six months in the county jail. Just before I was arrested we celebrated my daughter's seventh birthday. She did her math cards for me and got them all right. I was so proud of her that I cried. I rarely ever cried, and her grandmother later had to explain to my daughter that those were tears of joy from a proud dad who had to go away for a long time.

That's when I got some help, started reading the Bible, and took advantage of the treatment programs available. The programs were good. It's all about applying yourself. If you commit yourself to turning your life around you can do it.

My goal was to never go back to prison. My dad went down when I was eleven, and he got thirty years. I just found out he got out in 1989 after getting his case overturned. I've been trying to find him, but so far nothing has worked out.

What helped most in turning my life around was reading the Bible. Early on, my family had gone to church. That seed was planted many years ago.

The day I got out, I went to The NetWork for Better Futures. My younger brother worked there. While still in prison I had been in contact with Jeff Williams of The Network. He told me that if I was serious about turning my life around, they would have a bed and a job for me the day I got out. Now I have an apartment in my own name. For a long time I was living with girlfriends or the mothers of my kids. I was fooling around a lot. Now I have a place that I can call home. And I have full-time work thanks to Better Futures. So you see, there is no need to take a risk and go back on the street when you can go to work and have a guaranteed paycheck.

I have been out now for ten months, and every few weeks we have some bumps and bruises, but by the end of the week things get resolved and on Friday, at the end of the second week of work, I get a paycheck. There is a twenty-one-day orientation period, and then you get into the various work modules. Much of the work at The Network consists of stripping older appliances collected from aging apartment buildings and selling the valuable metals to recyclers. I learn something new every week—things like deconstruction, demolition, and construction—in addition to life skills such as parenting, social interaction, and managing finances. You must check in with your life skills coach each week. Some of the people in the program had never had a job and didn't know where to look for one or how to do an interview. Many are totally lost when they're released from prison. I did everything they told me to do and it has worked. As long as you're committed to change, they're behind you all the way.

I'm still on parole for another six months and then I'll be clear, and that will be a blessing. My children are with their mothers, and now that I have my own place I can have them on the weekends. I talk to my kids every day and have a good relationship with their moms. I work with them on their homework and want to keep them from taking the same path I did. I think that if I had had a real father who was there for me, things would have turned out better. I always liked sports and things like that but was never encouraged to go out there and do it. My son is nine and my daughter ten, and they're both active in sports and extracurricular activities.

That two and a half years away from my kids was just horrible. I didn't want them coming back and forth to the prisons so we stayed in touch by phone and with letters. I never really had any positive role models growing up. All my aunties and uncles wanted the fast money. They always had nice clothes, big cars, and fancy apartments. Most of them finally got their lives together. Most are working and some have their own business. I never say that I made mistakes in life but what I do say is that I have had a lot of life lessons. The key is how you deal with those lessons; the outcome depends on that.

I asked Lante whether good counselors during those middle school years when he was dropping out might have made a difference. He replied that at that time in his life, when he was kicked out of one school and then moved to another, it might have helped, but the intervention needed to come earlier. It's interesting how the impact of intervention and solid mentoring differs at different stages of a young person's life. In Lante's case, it appears that by middle school he had no conception of what it meant to be living a positive lifestyle with opportunities lying ahead for him.

During those middle school years there were people who cared, but I wasn't tuned into that; my mind was focused on other stuff. When I had this fight over a racial incident and was told not to come back to school without my mother, I now recognize that had I told her the truth, she would have helped me stay in that school rather than moving.

In hindsight the fight was stupid. My African American student buddies who had been at that school for some time felt that the new Asian kids were trying to take over the school. It all started in the lunch room over who controlled what table space. It was a real bad fight. It was a day when we were supposed to be mentoring the younger kids who would soon be coming into middle school. They saw the whole thing so we didn't set a very good example for them. I was the only student asked not to come back.

Lante added that having good counseling in the early high school years would also definitely have been a plus. When he went to North High School, students went off-campus for lunch, and he said that he would often go to a fast food place and simply not come back. He loved football, and with the right kind of support his athletic ability might have helped his academic performance. It's clear from Lante's comments that the lack of a positive male role model at home made a huge difference in his behavior. For those of us who have had positive role models, it's hard to comprehend the impact that not having one can have. In my own case, I can think of many positive models, including my mother and father, four older brothers, and numerous teachers.

My early years in grade school in Wisconsin were good ones, as well as my first year at Willard Hay in Minneapolis. I always had a good head on my shoulders. I just made a lot of very bad choices. It's strange how things change. When my dad brought my mom and us kids to Minnesota he was a sweetheart. Then it all changed. He started getting abusive and had taken her out of her element, which likely contributed to her drug habit. She eventually licked that. At the time, though, he was very abusive to the point where she was taken to the hospital. Yet when my older brother and sister tried to intervene, she cussed them out and defended my father. It was a strange scene for the rest of us to witness. That's why my older siblings left. They thought the entire scene was hopeless. My older brother still holds that over my mother, so they're not as close as a first child is supposed to be with his mother.

Since I've put prison behind me, the NetWork for Better Futures has been like family for me. I participate in all the meetings, go to community dinners, and speak out for them when asked. That's why I wanted to do this interview. It's good for me and it helps Better Futures. There are people out there just like me who need help, and I want to be part of getting them back on their feet. As to the future, as I mentioned earlier, I love to cook. My dream is to find a partner and open a restaurant some day. It's important to cook healthy foods so I'm baking more and frying less. My specialty is grilling! I know how to cook everything and love it when people enjoy my food.

As I said before, life is all about what you put into it. Some can talk a mile a minute but the results aren't there. It took me much too long to figure all that out, but now I know who I am and what I want to do with my life.

The social and economic costs of not providing good rehabilitative programs for ex-offenders is enormous. Annual prison costs average about $50,000 per year per inmate. The pre-arrest and court costs are in addition to that. Yet upon

their release, former prisoners receive minimal support with housing, job-skill training, or developing the social skills needed to survive on the outside. The NetWork for Better Futures is one of a handful of organizations attempting to fill that void. Steve Thomas created this organization, which, in addition to providing housing and life-skills learning, provides employment for ex-offenders. One of the business opportunities it sponsors involves reclaiming and recycling outdated household appliances, stripping them of valuable metals that can be resold. The process involves teamwork and a good deal of physical effort, teaching ex-offenders new skills, keeping them healthy, and increasing their chances for upward advancement.

John Pacheco

"This was the sixties, when there were riots on the north side of town, and the inner city neighborhoods were somewhat unstable. Most of the fights were between blacks and whites. We Hispanics sort of sat on the sidelines. Nevertheless, we thought it was important to look and act tough."

John Pacheco has seen the community from nearly every angle. From his time spent as a youth in detention facilities to an executive position with a leading Fortune 500 company, his leadership skills have touched nearly every key aspect of our community. He has seen the inside of both the non-profit and for-profit communities and brings a warm-hearted yet businesslike approach to helping the disadvantaged become self-sufficient. This is a story that to my mind best represents what is great about America. Young people can stumble for a while, but with enough energy and drive, and a bit of luck, there can be just enough tough love in the community to help them reach their full potential.

I was born and raised in Minneapolis. My grandmother and grandfather on both sides came from Mexico in the 1920s. My dad was born here in 1930. He grew up in south Minneapolis and my mother in north Minneapolis. I had three brothers and three sisters and a number of cousins living nearby. My father worked at Honeywell from the time he was nineteen until he retired at the age of fifty-eight. After the kids were all in school, my mother went to work for the Bureau of Engraving. My parents were both union members.

When I was three I contracted tuberculosis. In those days we all lived pretty close together, and tuberculosis came through the neighborhoods. I was sent to the Glen Lake Sanitorium for about a year and a half. Two of my cousins were also there. In the sanitorium I can remember rooms with rows of metal cribs. They would strap us in, so if you happened to climb over the rail you'd hang out on the side of the crib until they came back in the morning. They also put bells on our shoes so wherever we went, they could hear us walking. The belief then was that sunlight and fresh air would be helpful so they dressed us in diapers and let us run around outside. Now, of course, they use antibiotics. My mother and father never drove a car so they would come out on some weekends by bus to visit. So one of my earliest memories is of being locked up.

Even in my early years in the 1950s I didn't behave very well—or so I'm told. It was just a whole different environment for me coming out of the sanitorium. Our neighborhood was mostly Hispanic with many Native Americans. It was a lower-income area at that time, near Seven Corners, where the University of Minnesota law school is today. My folks rented and we moved around the area quite a bit. When I was in third grade my dad got tuberculosis and was also sent to the sanitorium, and we had to go on welfare. We would get our Christmas gifts from the Shriners and received assistance from other family members.

By the time I entered junior high school we had moved to the Phillips neighborhood, where I ran with a lot of the neighborhoods boys. We were always getting into trouble. This area around Franklin Avenue was populated by Native Americans, Latinos, African American, and poor whites. For me the discrimination I felt as a kid was because people thought I was Native American. When I went to the store the guy would ask, "What do you need, chief?" There were a lot of those things that got to me, so I was an angry young man for a long time.

I fought a lot in school, drank a lot, and committed crimes like stealing cars, breaking and entering, and assault. I'm not sure what was driving all that. I was just enjoying being a kid, I guess. Some days I would just get bored and I'd call someone and we'd hit the street. I wish I could blame all that on someone, but I can't. I came from a good family that worked hard and I also got lots of support from my siblings.

I think the first time I was arrested I was twelve or thirteen. We had broken into a Clark gas station to get whatever we wanted at that time. I was small so my friends would lift me up and slip me through the bars. Then I would open the door. As soon as we were in there we saw flashlights looking in the window, and we were taken to jail. In those days there were no juvenile facilities so you actually went to jail alongside adults.

I was then sent out to the Hennepin County home for boys in Glen Lake, which stood right next to my old sanitorium. I would be in and out of that county home repeatedly from seventh to tenth grade.

At Phillips Junior High the teachers were tough, but they were very collegial with the bad guys. They knew if you came to school dressed up you were more than likely going to court that day. When I got sent back out to Glen Lake for the second or third time the teachers would remind me to say hello to several of their former and current students.

My first time out to Glen Lake they brought me in a van, and as soon as I got there one of the guys greeted me and told me that my friend Jessie wanted to see me. He asked me what group I was in. They divided the kids up into groups called Knights, Black Hawks, Eagles, Vikings, and Spartans. You got assigned to these by age and size.

The bunk beds were all in a row. At night you were shoulder to shoulder in the shower and they told when and what part of you to wash in what order, and only then would they hand you a towel. Every day we got new t-shirts, one-size-fits-all boxer shorts, and socks. Every other day we got clean jeans. We attended assembly every morning and sat with our groups in the pews. Jessie had told me that Melvin and Norman ran my group, the Knights. He added that those were the guys to watch out for. Sure enough, the first day I showed up for assembly, Melvin put his foot up to block my way. In jail you learn fast to make it clear that you can't be messed with or else you really get stepped on. So I just wound up and hit him with everything I had. He was just sitting there in the pew and probably didn't even know my name. Another kid jumped over and came at me, and then Jessie and my friends stepped in and it became a real big deal. When Melvin came back from the infirmary he came down the hall and I hit him again. Then I was put in lock-up in a room with no bed for a while. After that no one ever bothered me again. Actually at that time I didn't mind fighting if I had to.

One summer I ran from there. We knew that if you followed the railroad tracks you could get back to the old neighborhood, so that's what we did. You had to be careful because the police also knew our route and were always on the lookout. So we traveled at night. I spent that summer sleeping in old boxcars and the like and fooling around during the day. Sometimes the police would come in looking for me and mistake my brother for me. It got to the point where my mom told me that I couldn't come around the house.

When summer ended I called my probation officer and asked, "What am I looking at in terms of jail time?" He said he was going to set a court date and if I showed up I would likely do up to a year at Glen Lake. Then he added that if they caught me, I would do at least a year in Red Wing. That's a much tougher institution. So I showed up in court and went back to the home school. I still knew lots of folks there because many were from my neighborhood.

Wrestling is what got me my first break at Glen Lake. One of the city coaches heard about me from a coach at Glen Lake because I was undefeated. I was asked to come to Vocational High, the school my father had graduated from. I asked if that would get me out of Glen Lake, and they said yes. Then they asked what I would like to study. I said that I wanted to be a machinist like my dad.

I started in January at Vocational High School in the middle of tenth grade. The rest of the kids had started in September. The way it works is that you start the day in your home room, then spend three hours in your trade area, and finish the day with the standard curriculum. But with me they just put me in the library for three hours and let the trade school part go until later. I wrestled for the school that year and finished the tenth grade with D minuses. By my senior year I was captain of the team and city champ in my weight class. I was the first from the school to qualify for the state and placed fourth. Then the letters started coming from colleges and universities. As soon as wrestling was over and I had won everything I could, Vocational kicked me out. I still had a year to make up in the machine shop, and they knew I was behind in all my other classes and wouldn't graduate on time. They had basically used me to wrestle and then cast me aside.

Now I'm out of school at age eighteen and know that I have credits to make up. I still ran around in the neighborhood but never got into drugs like many of my friends. It was kind of like counter–peer pressure. Most of my friends were either buying, selling, or using. My involvement with non-profits at that time was pretty limited. The first alternative school in Minneapolis was called The City Inc. My sister was one of the teen founders of the school, which was started by Father Joseph Selvaggio. My dad coached boxing there. They had pool tables, and it was a real safe place to be. I started boxing and won the Minneapolis Golden Gloves tournament.

This was the sixties, when there were riots on the north side of town, and the inner city neighborhoods were somewhat unstable. Most of the fights were between blacks and whites. We Hispanics sort of sat on the sidelines. Nevertheless, we thought it was important to look and act tough. It was the thing to do. I carried a .22 Baretta for a while but it scared me more than it was a threat to anyone else. Some guy did put a gun to my head once in a fight over a hat. By this time I was determined to stay out of jail. Too many of my friends were doing serious jail time as adults and I didn't want to join them.

I did well at The City Inc. and was able to get the necessary credits to get my diploma from Vocational. One of the teachers at The City helped me apply to the University of Minnesota and I was accepted in 1972. At the time I didn't realize what a big deal that was. I had a Martin Luther King Scholarship that paid

$300 per month and also covered my books. I was still moving around in the neighborhood and dropping in at The City Inc.

The university was hard for me. I would hitchhike to classes. I took several courses in social work. The Chicano movement was getting started in the early 1970s and there was group of young Chicanos fighting to establish the Chicano Studies Department at the University of Minnesota. They were successful in their efforts, and for me it served as an introduction to social activism and change. I was getting more interested in what I could do in the areas of social service and community activism related to social justice issues by then.

I received another break when, after school one day, I was playing pool at Mr. Nibs, a bar in south Minneapolis, and this guy walked in who was a counselor out at the county home for boys. His name was Curt Harstad. He asked me what I was doing and then told me that he had just started a halfway house on the university campus for convicted felons. He knew that I knew a bunch of those guys and offered me room and board plus $175 a month if I would serve as a counselor there after classes. Now I'm looking at $475 per month! I was surprised at his offer, considering that he knew my background. My job was basically to make sure no one destroyed the place. The guys who came there in 1973 were first-time offenders so the court had given them this option as an alternative to going to prison. They had to work or go to school, and my job, despite my lack of formal training, was to run the group therapy sessions. The model was called Positive Peer Culture, and I had already been exposed to the program at Glen Lake.

Some of these guys in the home were older and bigger than I was and thought they could push me around. I wasn't about to have any of that, so I recruited some guys I knew from jail who were good-sized and brought them into my group. They would support me when some of the other guys started to act up. As a result we had superb performance compared with some of the other programs, and when I was twenty-one they offered me a full-time position with pay at $27,000 a year! That was more money than I had ever dreamed about, so I left the U of M and took the job. That kept me busy for the next two years. Dave Nasby then hired me at The City Inc. to work with juveniles and serve as their legal advocate. I would meet with the kids' families and the probation officers and try to work out a program for them with the court. Everyone assumed that I had a legal degree because I was always well-dressed and knew how to conduct myself. The next year I was appointed to the University of Minnesota's Presidential Advisory Committee for the recruitment and retention of minority students. I served on that committee under three different presidents. Here I was doing all of this without having graduated from college!

One of the things I noticed was that people were listening to me. I went back and attended a few classes. Minneapolis Community College hired me at the same time I was at The City Inc. to teach a class on juvenile justice.

My next job was with a social action organization known as the Urban Coalition. Earl Craig was its executive director, and he had put a group together to look at public policy directed at low-income people of color. That's where I began to see the interrelationship between business, government, and the community. I also began to learn what advocacy and lobbying meant. Peter McLaughlin, now Hennepin County Commissioner, was head of their public research area. Steve Cramer, who has been on the Minneapolis City Council and ran Project for Pride in Living for many years, was the research assistant. Ron McKinley, a leader in the Native American community, was head of their outreach function. Luanne Nyberg, who later headed up the Minnesota Children's Defense Fund, was also involved in outreach. Vusi Zulu headed up their weatherization program. It was a most impressive team, and it was the experience of working with them that moved my attention from helping individual families to an understanding of how we can impact public policy to better the lives of many. My next job was as the executive director of Centro Cultural Chicano, a non-profit focused on supporting the Hispanic community. This got me involved in political campaigns, helping to establish the Minneapolis Police Civilian Review Panel and chairing the People of Phillips neighborhood council. Governor Rudy Perpich appointed me to the Juvenile Justice Advisory Committee and then to the Metropolitan Council. I thought about running for public office but stopped short of that and instead ran campaigns for other candidates.

My career moved to the corporate world when Merle Anderson, the director of government relations for Northern States Power Company, asked me to join his team, with responsibility for local government and community relations. My response was to let him know that I did not know anything about utilities, and in fact that I thought he had called me because I didn't pay my bill. After laughing, Merle explained that what he was try to do was strengthen the company's relationships at the local level. He believed my work in the community would make me a good fit to help him achieve that goal. Merle was right, and I learned a lot from him about corporate culture and giving back to communities. I later moved to a similar position at US Bank, and I continue to give back to the community personally through voluntary service on various non-profit boards.

John's contributions to his community cover a wide range of non-profit, for-profit, and government-related activities. These include serving on the boards of the Hennepin County Library System, the Metropolitan Sports Commission, and as the District 4 representative on the greater Twin Cities area Metropolitan Council. He has served as executive director of Centro (non-profit Latino social service agency) and director of the Hispanic AIDS Coalition (which implements HIV/AIDS prevention in the Latino Community). In 1991 he joined Northern States Power Company (now Xcel Energy) as manager of governmental affairs. Later, he became director of Xcel Energy's foundation and director of corporate citizenship. John joined US Bank in 2008 as director of the US Bank Foundation and Public Affairs, where he oversaw $25 million in annual philanthropic and community affairs efforts focused in the areas of economic opportunity, education, and arts and culture. In addition, he directed the company's United Way campaign with more than 220 bank entities generating $8.8 million in employee pledges and 65,000 employees who performed more than 260,000 hours of volunteer service.

It's interesting to note the different players who helped John along the way. Parents, teachers, parole officers, wrestling coaches, corrections counselors, non-profit executive directors, and for-profit human resource managers have each intervened at just the right moment to help John better his life. John, his mentors, and the community must take great pride in his remarkable success. In this case it was a community that helped raise a child to adulthood and to a postion where he could and did provide benefits for so many others both locally and nationally.

Tiffany Meeks

"So now I am having to think about baby food, child care, and all the supporting items you need to care for a young child. At age nineteen I was simply not prepared emotionally for all this."

I met with Tiffany Meeks in one of the conference rooms of the Carlson School of Business at the University of Minnesota, where she is employed as a program manager. The setting gave no indication of the struggle Tiffany had in getting there. I was interviewing an African American woman who represented her institution as a true professional. She was confident, knowledgeable, and relaxed as she welcomed me to the Carlson School.

I was born in Waterloo, Iowa, and in my early years lived with different relatives. My mom had me at age nineteen and wasn't prepared to raise a child. My dad was around, but my parents did not have a good relationship. I moved to Minnesota in 1986 with my mother and attended Minneapolis South High School. I did OK in school. After graduation I applied to St. Thomas University and was accepted. During my freshman year I became pregnant. That was scary and I wasn't sure what I wanted to do. Should I press forward or terminate the pregnancy? My mother was not supportive and thought my whole life was blowing up. I ended up deciding to keep my baby but had no idea of what I was getting myself into; I was nineteen. I had no idea of the costs involved and was not well-equipped to manage money in a responsible way. My mother's life was not stable and she was using drugs to medicate herself. This was an awakening.

I knew I wanted to finish college and also be a good mother to my daughter, showing her that no matter what challenges you face you can overcome them and be successful. I would have been the first female in my family to earn a college degree. My daughter, Natalie, was born in December of my freshman year, and after taking J term off I went back to school. So now I am having to think about baby food, child care, and all of the supporting items you need to care for a young child. We did receive some cash assistance, food stamps, and day care. There was a lot to manage and juggle, and when you're not prepared it makes life just that much harder. At age nineteen I was simply not prepared emotionally for all this. I was able to work part-time and go to school part-time, but finances continued to be a problem and my daughter and I wound up unable to afford a place to live.

Fortunately we avoided homelessness when a friend took us in. It was a small apartment with four other people and not a particularly safe place for my daughter. This was one of the lowest points in my life because I could see no way forward for us. I had lost all incentive to hope for a better future when a friend told me about Jeremiah Program. She had to call me a second time before I managed to put together an application. Then, out of the blue, one day they called and asked me to come in for an interview. I was keeping my expectations low. I interviewed with four women and told them about my situation and what my goals were. In September of 1998 I learned that I had been accepted. I cried because this meant that I could finish school and have a safe place for my child.

While I was at Jeremiah my rent was free and I was still able to go to school, work part time, and receive medical assistance and food stamps. One of the key programs there focused on life skills. We met in the evening, shared experiences, and learned more about parenting, empowerment, and health. The training in financial management was especially helpful. We learned from each other about how to save money and cut expenses. The program makes you feel like you can actually finish school, be a good parent, and become self-sufficient again. My daughter was three at the time. We moved into a two-bedroom furnished apartment with a living room and kitchen. The program at Jeremiah is thirty-six months long, and I moved out in the spring of 2001 after graduating from St. Thomas.

At Jeremiah there is this feeling of community where people can share experiences with others and get away from the loneliness that's often so much a part of their lives. The feeling of support there is strong since most of the women are dealing with the same issues that you are—trying to go to school and raise their kids at the same time. The staff is highly professional and they're there to support you in every way that they can. You have to take the initiative, but they will be there for you all the way. It felt very much like family.

My course work at St. Thomas was in business. I had classes in finance, economics, accounting, communication, management, marketing, statistics, and all the rest. There was even an opportunity at St. Thomas for me to study abroad in Ghana. When I finished at Jeremiah my kids were five and six. One was in preschool and the other in kindergarten. I had been working part time in retail, and after graduation I took a full-time job in their merchandising department. The transition to work was pretty easy for me. At $16 per hour we were able to do OK. We moved into an apartment in Richfield and we have been there ever since. Both of the kids have been in the Richfield schools. When my son was born there were medical complications, and I had to leave my retail job to be with him. Fortunately I was still with his father, whose job at one of the airlines helped us stay afloat financially. My daughter played basketball at Richfield and was in the state tournament two years in a row. She is now nineteen and studying graphic design at Robert Morris University in Chicago. I just love that!

After leaving my retail position I continued to work off and on in merchandising. I worked with United Health Care prior to my current job as a program manager for the Carlson School of Business.

As far as the future is concerned, my plan is to go back to school and get my MBA. It's clear that I wouldn't be where I am today without the Jeremiah Program. I continue to stay in touch with them and still consider them family.

One of the great limiting factors in helping struggling young single mothers get on the track towards self-sufficiency is the geographic fragmentation of our social service systems. Even if convenient transportation is available, the distance between home, work, and day care puts a nearly impossible burden on very-low-income families. How do young single mothers find time for educational opportunities that can lift them out of poverty? If they have come from dysfunctional families, where do they go for the basic counseling that can help them navigate our social service and educational systems? Father Michael O'Connell founded Jeremiah in 1998 with the purpose of providing

one-stop shopping for these young mothers where quality day care, affordable housing, and counseling allowed them to educate themselves. By bringing these essential support elements together under one roof, Jeremiah helps single mothers, after thirty months in the program, find work paying in excess of $15 an hour on average.

Epilogue

As you could tell from following the lives of the individuals described in this book, none can claim they were not helped along the way by some individual or group. In some cases it was a spiritual awakening at a quiet moment, in others a wake-up call to the responsibility of caring for themselves and their families. In still others it was gratitude for coming to a land where they could be out of harm's way. These stories represent men and women with African, Asian, Hispanic, Native American, African America and European backgrounds. In many cases the assistance came at just the right time.

Clearly, the timing of helpful interventions is important. With the benefit of hindsight we can say that early intervention is the most effective. One of the greatest challenges has been the harmful legacy of generational poverty and racism that has haunted young African Americans, especially where there are no positive male role models at home. Memories of parents and siblings lost through civil war as well as physical and mental abuse create enormous challenges for immigrants who come to a new land with little knowledge of the language.

We have also learned that even in some of our most supportive families young people can make mistakes that put them in a dangerous downward spiral. Taken together, the stories in this book illustrate the broad range of knowledge and skill required by non-profits and professionals who are dedicated to helping individuals become productive citizens. Often it is simply the art of listening and knowing what remedy or service agency to recommend that creates a winning situation.

We are blessed with a wide array of these organizations, and they perform miracles each day. Not only are they doing what is fair and just and right, but over time they offer tremendous economic value when they can convert someone embroiled in social services or the criminal justice system to becoming productive employees and taxpayers. The work these organizations do is essential to our future economic health, as leading economists and demographers continue to projected a severe shortage of skilled and semi-skilled workers in the decades ahead.

To illustrate the wide range of support services available and how agencies must often work together to help someone gain self-sufficiency, I would like to share with you the story of one refugee who was abused and tortured and came to this country nearly penniless. (Because of possible harm coming to members of his family still in Africa the individual's name has been changed.)

Mario Owusu came to this country at age thirty-five, not speaking English and physically and emotionally unable to work. Mario grew up in Sudan in East Africa. He arrived in the United States in 2004 seeking asylum. After being welcomed to the United States by Lutheran Social Services he was immediately referred to the Center for Victims of Torture, which is based at the University of Minnesota. Seeking asylum is a long and difficult process and his was only finalized in 2006 with the assistance of Minnesota Advocates for Human Rights.

Mario had been an outspoken advocate for human rights

before being imprisoned and severely tortured. When his health returned he began training in English with a local non-profit and then went to work doing maintenance chores in a church near his apartment. The work was full-time, six days a week.

A workforce development organization called Twin Cities Rise was his next commitment. Here he learned the full range of soft and hard skills necessary for finding and holding a living-wage job. At this time Mario was renting a room in a home in Burnsville, a suburb of Minneapolis, for $450 per month and earning $850 per month.

His next step was to take a financial class at Lutheran Social Services that dealt with accounting, budgeting, and different saving and investment options. He took advantage of a grant program there that would match three times whatever he saved in one year up to $3,000. While still only earning $800 a month, Mario was able to save $100 per month for ten months. Transportation was still a headache for him, however, because work, housing, and after-hours schooling were all in different parts of the city. He became a master of local bus schedules.

With $4,000 in the bank, Mario was unsure what his next step should be. A friend suggested he contact the Minneapolis City of Lakes Land Trust. They told him that he needed additional income to qualify for their program. He took the message to heart and found work with a non-profit paying $11.50 per hour. He visited a local bank and applied for a loan, and was told he would qualify for a mortgage if he could make a $55,000 down payment. City of Lakes Land Trust agreed to make the down payment if Mario could find an appropriate home. He found a home in north Minneapolis putting up the $4,000 he still had in the bank. The mortgage payment was $750 per month for a good-sized timber framed home with four bedrooms and one and one half baths.

Owning the house has made it possible for Mario to bring his immediate family and a few members of his extended family to Minneapolis, where they now all live under one roof. He credits five non-profit organizations and a host of caring neighbors for his success.

This story and the others are but a small sample of the remarkable work being done each day by our leading non-profit organizations.

What follows is a listing and description of the organizations represented in *Turnabout*.

Further Information about the Civic Organizations Referred to in These Stories

THE ADVOCATES FOR HUMAN RIGHTS

The Advocates for Human Rights has been assisting individuals in realizing their human rights in the United States and around the world for more than thirty years. The Advocates' services have aided refugees and immigrants, women, ethnic and religious minorities, children, and others whose basic freedoms and rights are at risk. The Advocates has prepared and published seventy-five reports documenting human rights abuses and practices in twenty-five countries, thus raising awareness of the work that needs to be done.

The Advocates works locally with organizations to document human rights abuses against women, including employment discrimination, rape, domestic violence, sexual harassment in the workplace, and sex trafficking in women and girls. The organization has long promoted human rights locally and globally through advocacy, research, and education. The Advocates runs a Discover Human Rights Institute that provides educational resources for teachers, students, lawyers, and other social justice advocates, and invites them to "join us in building a world in which the human rights of everyone, everywhere, are respected."

The Advocates have been given Special Consultative Status by the United Nations, which allows them to participate in regional human rights programs. This permits outreach to professional volunteers who can expand The Advocates international advocacy efforts.

United Nations advocacy by the Advocates includes statements to charter-based organizations such as the Human Rights Council, participation in United Nations reviews of compliance with human rights treaties, and providing technical advice. International fact-finding missions document violations of the economic and social rights of children and rights violations in the administration of justice. Reports also cover topics such as the harassment of human rights defenders, police and military abuses, and restraints on freedom of the press.

AFRICAN DEVELOPMENT CENTER

The African Development Center (ADC) is an economic development organization and commercial lender with the mission to grow businesses, build wealth, and increase investment in Minnesota's African communities. This is accomplished by business development activities, homebuyer workshops, and financial literacy training.

ADC was founded in 2004 with three employees and now has ten. The first loan of $25,000 was granted in May of 2005. When ADC started making loans, the mix was 60 percent for start-ups and 40 percent for on-going businesses; today the mix is 90 percent and 10 percent respectively. The current ADC portfolio includes more than two hundred clients and more than $5 million in loans. ADC is working to help African immigrants develop skills and access to resources to assist them in owning homes and businesses at the same rate as long-time Minnesotans.

ADC's programs and tools include business development services such as planning workshops and technical assistance; business financing, including micro-lending; home-ownership training; and financial literacy counseling. Because of the ADC's reputation and experience in micro-lending, the SBA designated them as an official micro-lender. ADC is also serving greater Minnesota with offices in Rochester and Willmar. Minnesota Community Foundation also awarded a transformational grant of $410,000 to support a new ADC social venture, ADC Business Consulting. Since 2004 more than four-hundred jobs have been created or sustained because of ADC loans and programs.

ADC has addressed issues within the Islamic community concerning the payment of interest. ADC helps Muslim and non-Muslim borrowers finance their businesses using a profit-based financing system. ADC agrees to buy business equipment or inventory on behalf of the borrower and then resells the equipment or inventory to the borrower at the original cost plus profit. Payments are made on monthly installments over a 36- to 60-month period. As these entrepreneurs live longer in the U.S. they become less committed to religious beliefs and more concerned with lower-cost financing. Consequently, in the last several years there has been a huge shift to conventional financing by this community.

BETTER FUTURES MINNESOTA

The organization has taken on the mission of challenging the current practices of the criminal justice system that are too often meant to supervise, punish, and treat ex-offenders as men who have locked themselves out of opportunities in mainstream society and entered a perpetual cycle of violence, dependency, unemployment, homelessness, emergency care, and incarceration. As a social enterprise BFM describes its mission as looking through the lens of public health and building a movement that supports personal transformation and the building of a healthy, vibrant community of men. The mission is to fuel and guide men's desire to turn their lives around and walk a new path toward better health and success.

Better Futures works with men directly out of prison who are committed to changing their lives. Since prison generally leaves these men with no more than $100 plus whatever they earned while they were locked up, the transition to mainstream society is difficult, to say the least. The Better Future model calls for a four-step process that involves finding temporary housing, life-skills coaching, practicing healthy lifestyles, and receiving job-skill training. Dealing with the trauma of their earlier lives and adopting healthy behavioral practices requires a supportive culture that helps men achieve a new identity and sense of self-esteem.

When the fundamentals are in place, a process is set in motion that transforms clients from social dependents to positive, revenue-generating members of families and society. Participants continue at BFM by paying full rent, finding and keeping a full-time job, paying child support and any restitution, securing a valid ID or driver's license, serving as a peer mentor, attending all community meetings, avoiding new criminal activity or release violations, and opening a bank account and saving at least $1000.

Typical work might involve the demolition of old buildings and recycling building materials. Other contracts are bid to remove old appliances from apartment buildings and then tear them apart so that copper, aluminum, steel, and other metals can be recycled. The men acquire deconstruction skills while also learning how to negotiate contracts and complete assignments on schedule.

More than 80 percent of the men who enroll are homeless. Nearly all of them are African American, and only 5 percent have jobs. On average during the course of a year the program may enroll more than two-hundred men. Each enrollee is assisted with housing, and nine out of ten find jobs. A majority of the men are then able to make their child support payments. More than 70 percent obtain health care insurance.

THE CENTER FOR VICTIMS OF TORTURE

The Center for Victims of Torture (CVT) was founded in 1985 as an independent non-governmental organization dedicated to meeting the needs of torture survivors. Care is provided in a residential settings designed to create a healing environment. Key activities include healing therapies, training, research, advocacy, and the publication of survivor stories. In addition to treating torture survivors in Minnesota and the rest of the United States, CVT has established a presence in the Middle East, Africa, and other countries where torture is prevalent.

International work began in Bosnia and Croatia in 1993. As the war continued, CVT psychotherapists went to the region to train care providers in the highly specialized treatment of torture survivors. Work began in Turkey in 1995 to improve the skills of medical professionals and non-governmental organizations that support torture survivors.

CVT launched its first international direct healing program in Guinea, West Africa, in 1999, working with refugees from Sierra Leone. Mental heath counseling was provided to refugees who had experienced torture and trauma during the many conflicts in the area. Residents of the refugee camps were trained as paraprofessional psychosocial peer counselors by CVT psychotherapists. These peer mental health counselors continued to support a local mental health network after completion of the program in 2005.

Direct care has also been extended by CVT to refugees returning to the Democratic Republic of the Congo, refugees of the Somali war in the Dadaab camps in northern Kenya, urban refugees in Nairobi, Kenya, Iraqi and Syrian refugees in Jordan, and Eritrean refugees in northern Ethiopia.

With respect to advocacy, CVT has worked with faith-based groups to secure nearly $400,000 for the United Nations Fund for Victims of Torture, a program that provides financial support to torture survivor rehabilitation centers worldwide. In addition, CVT was instrumental in passing the Torture Victims Relief Act. Since the year 2000 the United States has been the world's largest donor to torture survivor rehabilitation.

THE CITY, INC.

In the fall of 1967, a group of fathers and sons met with father Joseph Selvaggio, a priest from the city's Holy Rosary Church, to try to solve community issues associated with youth behavior in the area. Space was rented on the city's south side to hold social functions and to give young people a place to meet after school. Originally called the Psychotic City Teen Center, its purpose was to serve as an agent for healing, growth, and advocacy for inner-city young people and their families. Later, space was also made available in the heart of one of the more troubled neighborhoods in north Minneapolis.

The name was soon changed to The City, Inc. Social services

were added in 1980, and a school was opened offering a curriculum that included English, science, social studies, fine arts, vocational education, and math. More recently, classes have been offered in computer science and construction, along with a broader post-secondary counseling system.

The City received funding primarily through the United Way. Its goal was to create hope, search out opportunity, and build a sense of community in the young people, families, and communities it serves. During its nearly forty-five years in operation, The City Inc. demonstrated that alternative schools shaped to the needs of the local neighborhood could have a transformative effect on young people whose learning style required new and more user-friendly techniques to create an interest in education. Annual enrollment averaged about seventy-five students. The model has been replicated in other neighborhoods and served as a valuable resource in the development of the charter school movement.

City of Lakes Community Land Trust

The formation of community land trusts is accelerating nationally as a vehicle to make home ownership affordable to low- and moderate-income families. The concept involves freezing, to the extent possible, a significant portion of the increases in the cost of home ownership over a very long period of time. Historically the gap continues to widen between the cost of housing and the wages earned by the average household. When families pay more than 30 percent of their income for housing, the family is stressed financially and moves frequently in search of affordable rent. This, in turn, affects school performance, job performance, child care costs, and transportation logistics. Substandard housing impacts family health, results in overcrowding, and often increases the chances an individual will run foul of the law.

The City of Lakes Community Land Trust (CLCLT), which serves Minneapolis residents, evolved from a collaboration of local neighborhoods that began in late 2001 and includes Powderhorn Residents Group, Seward Redesign, Powderhorn Park Neighborhood Association, and Lyndale Neighborhood Development Corporation. CLCLT provides permanently affordable housing for low- to moderate-income home buyers by owning the land but selling the home on the land to an income-qualified buyer. It does this by bringing an affordability investment, typically ranging from 20 to 50 percent of the total property cost, to assist the homeowner in the purchase. The CLCLT then assigns this affordability investment to the title of the land to ensure the home will remain perpetually affordable. The homeowner then leases the land through a renewable ground lease. When the homeowner sells the house, their equity plus 25 percent of the appreciated value is returned to them, and 75 percent of the appreciated value remains with CLCLT to make the same home affordable to future buyers. It is estimated that more than 170,000 low-income Twin Cities area households are currently paying more than they can afford for housing. Many are renters who are not building equity through home ownership. In addition, an estimated 20,000 or more households lack affordable housing in the Twin Cities metropolitan area. While 35 percent of Minneapolis residents are people of color, only 15 percent are "communities of color" homeowners.

College Possible

Admission Possible was founded in September 2000 to enable students who had never entertained thoughts of attending college the opportunity to develop the skills needed to gain admission to a four-year institution of higher learning. The organization began by serving thirty-five students in the Twin Cities, and over the past decade it has served nearly ten thousand low-income high school juniors and seniors in the metropolitan area. It has had a remarkable record in a short period of time. Low-income families offer a rich untapped source of future college graduates because historically their rate of college attendance has been very low and demographically their anticipated future growth rate is comparatively high. Typically, children from these families have little chance of going to college without intervention by a caring and knowledgeable third party. The cost of successfully mentoring these students, the increased probability of their gaining college admission and graduation, and the significantly increased lifetime earnings for college graduates are key inputs in documenting the great economic value of this program.

Admission Possible utilizes AmeriCorp coaches to deliver its services. These full-time mentors provide personal coaching to ten to fifteen students at each high school. Coaches also meet with the same group of juniors and seniors two afternoons per week for two hours. Students participate in a total of about 320 hours over two years on group ACT preparation, group admissions and financial aid counseling, and one-on-one admissions and financial aid consulting visits. Personal coaching continues over the summer, with students expected to apply for a summer enrichment program. College graduates on average have lifetime earnings of about $2,300,000 ($60,000/year), which is roughly twice what those with only a high school diploma can expect to earn: $1,240,000 ($30,000/year).

Demographic projections show a decline in the number of college graduates over the next two decades. This has serious negative implications for the growth of the U.S. workforce. The only college-age population expected to grow over the next ten to twenty years is that of minority students, including African American and Hispanic students. Students from these populations come disproportionately from low-income families where parents likely did not attend college. This poses substantial barriers to their chances of going to college. The U.S. Department of Education reports that higher-income students who scored in the top third of a standardized test are five times more likely to attend college than lower-income students with comparable scores. The benefits of advancing more high school students of color to a college education are substantial. The first to gain advantage are the students themselves, who gain a lifetime earnings advantage of more than $1,000,000 over their non-college -bound friends. Next are the employers, who will face a critical shortage of skilled workers over the next two decades. Finally, taxpayers gain as students become taxpayers and enhance their incomes through career advancement.

COMMON BOND COMMUNITIES

Common Bond Communities (CBC) is Minnesota's largest non-profit provider of affordable housing, serving nearly 9,000 residents in more than 5,500 affordable apartments and townhomes. CBC has pioneered the concept of "affordable housing linked to services" with remarkable success. Residents reside in 104 properties located in Minnesota, Iowa, and Wisconsin. The annual budget exceeds $20 million, which is substantially funded by earned income. Historically, affordable housing providers have been in the bricks-and-mortar business, constructing and managing rental properties. Experience has shown that housing must be effectively linked with human services if low-income people with special needs are to have the resources to become self-reliant.

The Advantage Center service delivery model within Common Bond has been delivering services to senior citizens, many of whom are at risk, for more than twenty years, as well as to working-age heads of households, including many who are single mothers, and their children. Among these clients are increasing numbers of working poor, people with mental and physical challenges, and refugees and immigrants. The long-term goal is to help heads of households find and hold jobs with benefits so they can move on to market-rate rental or home ownership. Other goals are to ensure that school-age children have a regular adult role model so that they can achieve their highest academic potential, and to train senior citizens to live independently in their own homes. Core programs include Career Advantage, which assists residents in finding and keeping living-wage jobs with benefits; Study Buddies, where consistent one-on-one mentoring for at-risk youth aims to enhance academic achievement; Customized Services Coordination, which stabilizes families by increasing access to community-based educational and service resources; Computer Labs, which helps close the digital divide between rich and poor; and Community Boards and Resident Associations that enrich lives, generating a sense of ownership along with leadership, volunteer service, and recreational opportunities.

High School for Recording Arts

High School for Recording Arts (HSRA) is a public charter high school located in the Midway neighborhood of St. Paul, Minnesota. The nickname Hip-Hop High refers to the fact that the school pioneered the notion of attracting at-risk students by offering a hip-hop music program.

The school opened in 1996 as a pilot program for at-risk students interested in a career in music. In addition to standard classroom space, the school operates two professional recording studios. The school can accommodate 250 students.

Daily required courses include language, arts, and mathematics, along with interdisciplinary programs that relate traditional academics with practical, real-world, experiential learning. Each student has his or her own personalized learning plan. HSRA graduates must meet all state requirements for graduation, present a portfolio summarizing learning in twelve core areas, complete a college acceptance letter, describe their post–high school plans, and submit samples of their work.

The demographic makeup is 59 percent male and 41 percent female. The average enrollment age is nineteen. Ninety-two percent of students are at or below the poverty level, and 30 percent have been homeless. Eighty-six percent are black, 6 percent Caucasian, 4 percent Hispanic, 4 percent Native American, and 0.3 percent Asian. In terms of geography, 81 percent of the students come from the Twin Cities and 19 percent from other parts of Minnesota.

HIRED

HIRED was founded in 1968 by former criminal justice system offenders, executives from Honeywell Corporation, and other private-sector firms to assist individuals released from prison to relocate and find living-wage jobs. It has a full range of services for adults and youth seeking employment in the Twin Cities. More than 11,000 job-seekers are enrolled at HIRED each year. On average, employment counselors place more than 3,300 youth and adults in jobs each year at an average wage of $15.51 per hour. Performance measures include job placements, starting wages, job retention, assignments to vocational training, and diploma or GED completion. The cost per placement ranges from $2,000 for a youth placement to $4,000 for an adult placement. The average wage at placement ranges from $8.36 for at-risk youth to $11.86 for disadvantaged adults to $22.45 for dislocated workers.

Key programs include Welfare to Work, for low-income parents; Dislocated Worker Training and Placement; Youth Employment; and Employer Services. HIRED's Job Link is a computerized job-posting system currently used by more than 3,500 Twin Cities employers. HIRED operates its programs through sixteen community-based, full-service offices across the Twin City metropolitan area in collaboration with public schools, correctional facilities, and a wide range of other employment service providers. The staff of 126 professionals is fluent in twenty languages, reflecting the growing impact of refugees and immigrants on the area's workforce. Services to refugees commenced in 1979, requiring a more diverse staff and new emphasis on training in the areas of workforce culture and literacy. Initially serving the state's growing southeast Asian refugee programs, HIRED now helps immigrants from Mexico, Somalia, the former Soviet Union, Myanmar, Laos, and Turkey, among others.

HIRED has three programs designed to meet the educational and employment needs of young parents. They are the Young Adult Program, working with Ramsey County helping low-income parents find jobs and transition off public assistance; Program for Academic and Career Excellence (PACE), which assists young parents in completing high school, getting a GED, or locating a job-training program, all while still parenting their children; and Teen Hope, which works in partnership with the MN Visiting Nurse Agency to help eighteen- and nineteen-year-old parents stay in school and ensure a safe and stable home environment. Young parents may achieve incredible outcomes despite having a number of barriers such as mental health issues, violent or abusive partners, limited work histories, unreliable transportation, and unstable housing.

JEREMIAH

The Jeremiah Program was launched in 1998 by the Rev. Michael O'Connell with the acceptance of eighteen families into residence. Jeremiah today is a leading innovator in providing supportive services to chronically homeless single mothers and their children. The enrollees' journey to self-reliance begins with what Jeremiah calls Foundational Support, which calls for safe and secure housing, quality early childhood education, and a sustainable and supportive community. Building upon that base are programs for skill and vision building, which involve empowerment experiences, job skills, and life skills. This sets the stage for post-secondary education, which in turn opens the door for gainful employment.

With facilities in Minneapolis, St. Paul, Fargo/Moorhead, and Austin, Texas, Jeremiah operates with a professional staff of thirty. Key operating functions include directors of family services, child development, life-skills coaching, strategic partnerships, volunteerism admissions, and alumni relations. Life-skills coaches who work with single mothers are housed at each location. Other key functions are headed by directors of advancement and finance/administration.

The program serves low-income single mothers with children who are under age five at the time of application. Families come from unstable housing, with about 30 percent coming from homeless shelters. Mothers are at least eighteen years of age, must have a high school diploma or GED, and be accepted to or enrolled in a vocational or other post-secondary training program. Children are enrolled in the on-site Child Development Center, where they engage in social, emotional, intellectual, and physical development activities. Classrooms house children ages infant to five. The organization partners with educational institutions, non-profit organizations, congregations, corporations, and a number of community groups for specific services that support resident families.

Women enter the program earning $8.39 an hour on average and graduate within two and one half years earning $16–$17 an hour. Many have relied upon public assistance and have not paid taxes. Part of the curriculum involves learning how to manage debt and practice good financial management. Sixty percent of graduates earn at a minimum an Associate of Arts degree, and 40 percent earn a four-year degree. Graduates are able to afford safe housing, and 30 percent become homeowners. Many of the children have experienced extreme levels of poverty. Graduates who were willing to share information report that their children are now performing at age-appropriate developmental levels.

THE LEGAL RIGHTS CENTER

The Legal Rights Center (LRC) represents, without charge, low-income people and people of color who have legal problems associated with the juvenile justice, criminal justice, and child welfare systems. LRC attorneys, community workers, and mediators are committed to protecting their clients' constitutional rights while assisting with the personal and social issues that often lead to the need for legal services. By addressing the broader problems, LRC seeks to restore the alleged offender to meaningful community life and reduce the likelihood of re-involvement with the juvenile or criminal justice system or the child welfare system. LRC's success will result in an increase in the quality of justice for low-income people and people of color and a decrease in the social costs associated with criminal behavior. The geographical focus of LRC's work is Hennepin County, Minnesota.

LRC is a community-driven nonprofit law firm specializing in criminal defense, both adult and juvenile, and restorative justice practices and advocacy. Community-driven refers to the diversity of staff and board, and also to the distinctive bottom-up internal structure in which community advocates, rather than attorneys, take the lead in assessing community needs, setting up defense representation with the center's staff attorneys, and helping with referrals to other social service agencies.

In 2008, the Legal Rights Center began a partnership with the Minneapolis Public Schools in which restorative justice became a lifeline to graduation for students who had been recommended to the district for expulsion. Using an innovative adaptation of the Family Group Conferencing method, the Legal Rights Center supports students, parents, and schools all working together to make sure the youth's mistake does not permanently undermine his or her education and life opportunities. The project constitutes a strategic shift in the Legal Rights Center towards preventing young men and women from getting involved in the juvenile justice system. The benefits quickly became apparent, and the project responded to the increased demand by doubling its capacity in its second year.

LOCAL INITIATIVES SUPPORT CORPORATION

The national Local Initiatives Support Corporation (LISC) celebrated its thirtieth anniversary in 2010 and now has thirty local affiliates, including Twin Cities LISC and rural programs. It was founded in 1979 with support from the Ford Foundation. LISC is a financial and community development intermediary that bridges various community sectors with partnerships between private, public, and non-profit organizations to provide economic, physical, and human capital by means of initiatives that support developers, train individuals, engage the community, provide financing for capacity building and operational support, grow leadership, and provide systems support in the area of policy. LISC provides pre-development financing with non-profits "early in the deal," technical assistance, tax-credit-based equity financing, acquisition lending, and feasibility grants. LISC tends to provide grants and loans in development instances where banks are not comfortable with the level of risk.

The local LISC organization has been in the Twin Cities for twenty-five years. It started out in St. Paul but ten years later began to fund projects in Minneapolis. During this period Twin Cities LISC has made nearly $500 million in grants, loans, and equity investment; made $1.8 billion in leveraged investments; funded 1.6 million square feet of commercial and community space; and participated in the creation of about 12,000 homes and apartments. Twin Cities LISC has a long history of success at leveraging funds. For every local $1 invested in Twin Cities LISC, they are able to invest an additional $10 in Twin Cities' neighborhoods.

Early on, a key goal of LISC was to "help residents and community-based organizations rebuild blighted neighborhoods to improve their quality of life." More recently, the focus has been on "building sustainable communities." This is done by focusing on five goals: 1) support healthy environments and lifestyles; 2) expand real estate investments; 3) increase family income and wealth; 4) stimulate economic activity; and 5) improve access to quality education. This new approach is "not just grants, loans, and equity" but involves a "layering of support" in the areas of leadership development; relationship brokering; the convening of people, projects, and initiatives; and policy advocacy. As part of Twin Cities LISC's new strategic plan, the organization is committed to investing and leveraging $30 million in grants and loans over the next three years to build sustainable communities.

LUTHERAN SOCIAL SERVICES

Since 1865, Lutheran Social Services has responded to the needs of Minnesota residents. Serving each of Minnesota's eighty-seven counties, LSS staff of 2,300 directly serve more than 75,000 people in more than 300 communities. Services are organized around children, youth, people with disabilities, and senior citizens. The range of services provided is broad, including the following:

adoption
camps, retreat centers and event venues
caregiver support and respite services
consumer directed community support services
counseling and support services
crisis nurseries and shelters for youth
disaster responses and recovery services
education, training and support groups
employment services
financial counseling and debt management
foster care
guardianship and conservatorship services
health care, treatment and rehabilitation
homeless youth services
housing services
meals for seniors
older adult volunteer program
parenting services
pooled trusts for people with disabilities
pregnancy counseling and birthparent services
refugee services
residential and in-home support services
the center for changing livesveteran and military family services

The Minneapolis Urban Coalition

This organization was formed following the riots in north Minneapolis during the mid-1970s. Near north neighborhoods felt left out of the economic and social gains following World War II, as evidenced by high concentrations of African Americans living in poverty. Minneapolis civic leaders organized dialogues between business executives, elected officials, and near north residents and came up with a series of recommendations related to racism, housing, education, job-skill training, fairer police conduct, court procedures, and a renewed commitment to listen to and act upon the concerns of near north residents. The organization developed a professional staff that researched key community issues and implemented new initiatives in partnership with corporate and civic leaders. A by-product of the Urban Coalition was the education and deveopment of a host of civic leaders who later went on to elected positions in city, county, and state offices.

Neighborhood Development Center

NDC is a community-based non-profit organized to "empower entrepreneurs and community partners to transform their low-income neighborhood economies from within." NDC surveys neighborhood groups, small businesses, and residents in communities to determine who has the knowledge, energy, and skill to revitalize their own neighborhoods. Prospective entrepreneurs of color and low-income residents in the Twin Cities who want to open or expand their business are encouraged to attend workshops describing the challenges and opportunities of participating in the NDC program.

Working with neighborhood organizations, NDC offers micro-entrepreneurial training in small groups in the participants' local areas. Training is twenty weeks long with classes lasting for two hours, followed by one-on-one training for an additional hour. Training is culturally geared to Somali, Latino, Hmong, East African, and American Indian entrepreneurs and draws upon the relevant peer groups and languages.

Technical assistance is available after a business gets started or expands and can include business plan revisions, web-based and traditional marketing, graphic design and branding, financial management. and more specialized assistance in areas such as restaurant management. Alumni business owners get a listing in the annual business directory and have access to pro bono legal services, networking opportunities, and joint marketing initiatives.

NDC also supports business incubators where businesses can get organized and develop in a shared environment that lowers costs and provides group marketing opportunities and support for ongoing business challenges. Incubators are currently located in seven Twin Cities locations. Since 1993 more than 4,200 businesses have been assisted by NDC, with entrepreneurs now running more than 460 businesses that in the aggregate contribute in excess of $70 million annually to the Twin Cities area economy.

Summit Academy OIC

Summit Academy OIC is a workforce training organization offering both soft and hard skills training. Its core philosophy is that "the best welfare program is a job." It largely serves the minority community, with 90 percent of the student body comprising African American males in the twenty-six-to-thirty-five age group. The pipeline into SAOIC is fed by word of mouth. Acceptance into the twenty-week program is based on assessments by SAOIC staff, including tests on math and reading. After acceptance, a mandatory level of attendance of 85 percent is required. SAOIC has expectations in the areas of dress (no sideways caps, low-rider pants, or colors), deportment in the building, and classroom behavior. Eighty percent of the students who are accepted make it through the program. The skills training focuses on healthcare services, nine construction areas leading to apprenticeship (plumbing, painting, carpentry, electrical, etc.), heavy equipment operation, truck driving, weatherization, and residential rehabilitation training. Specialized skills-development training is delivered based on partnerships with unions such as the IBEW. Hands-on training in heavy equipment operation, after initial classes at SAOIC, takes place at a large training site in Hinckley, Minnesota.

Ninety percent of the current enrollment is in the construction trades. In order to place graduates in construction jobs, CEO Louis King meets with contractors to request that they meet contractual goals for minority hiring. He has also raised the issue with the Minnesota Department of Transportations regarding its lack of enforcement of minority hiring goals with its contractors. In the past he has worked on minority hiring for the construction of the Minnesota Twins Target Field, the St. Paul Saints ballpark, and for construction of the new Vikings stadium.

In the construction area students study print reading, pricing, green construction, OSHA 30, and working with tools. This training lasts for twenty weeks and is split into two ten-week phases. The first ten weeks focuses on core competency, with the end result being "job ready." The second ten weeks involves "hands on" training to master technical skills. Small-scale model homes are built and then completely deconstructed down to raw materials. The students learn demolition techniques that don't destroy the materials. Program funding comes from both private and government sources.

THINK SMALL

Think Small was organized in St. Paul, Minnesota, in 1971, at a time when mothers of young children were entering the workforce in record numbers. The issue at the time was to provide care for their children at reasonable cost. Starting initially as a mobile toy-lending library, Think Small, through growth and merger, has become a large, multi-faceted child care advocacy and education center, with a database of more than 5,200 programs to give parents accurate information and consultation to help them get the child care that best meets their needs. The organization also offers professional development for early childhood practitioners in fifty-two communities. Classes and workshops build skills in delivering high-quality care and managing successful child care businesses. The curriculum includes topics on child development, curriculum planning, program assessment, parent and provider relationships, and health and safety. On average, 11,000 students are enrolled with multi-lingual classroom course offerings totaling 2,000 hours. The organization also offers career guidance for certification.

Direct service is provided to English language learners, new Americans, immigrant families, and underserved communities to engage families in Minnesota's child care and education systems. A range of languages are spoken, including Hmong, Spanish, Amharic, Somali, and Oromo. On-site, one-on-one services are offered to children with emotional and behavioral challenges and special needs.

Think Small manages about $4.4 million in scholarship program funds for families to enroll children in Parent Aware quality-rated programs. Think Small manages three financial support programs for providers and families: quality improvement grants and emergency funding for early childhood programs based on citizen reviewer recommendations, an eligibility-based scholarship pilot program for families to enroll children in programs rated high by the Minnesota Parent Aware Quality Rating System, and basic sliding-fee child care assistance for eligibility-based low-income families in Ramsey County. Last year, Think Small administered $1.3 million in scholarship and allowance funds, provided 350 quality-improvement grants to early childhood programs, and administered child care assistance to 1,155 low-income families in Ramsey County.

Advocacy efforts have resulted in Minnesota adopting an Early Childhood Education Center Rating System as well as funding to permit low-income families to use the rating system to find appropriate centers for their children. Minnesota State Early Learning Scholarships give families financial support up to $5,000 to help pay for high-quality early care and education, the better to prepare their young children for school.

Who can be in the program?

- Families living in Aitkin, St. Louis, Carlton, Scott, Washington, Anoka, Hennepin, Ramsey, Carver, Itasca, or Dakota Counties.
- Families with a child who is between the ages of three and five and not yet eligible for kindergarten, and
- Families who have an annual income at or below 185 percent of the Federal Poverty Guideline, based on the 2013 Federal Poverty Guidelines chart.

TWIN CITIES RISE!

Founded in 1994 by former General Mills executive Steve Rothschild, Twin Cities RISE! (TCR!) offers a high return on investment to its sponsors. TCR! fills a gap in the continuum for training and educating individuals. It provides intensive skills training for the very hard-to-employ poor not served by many non-profit placement programs or institutions of higher education. Its unique market-based training serves the employer as its customer, insuring that its graduates fill needed jobs at living wages. Graduates can earn living wage salaries of $22,000 or higher. TCR!'s impressive retention rate of 82 percent through 12 months on the job and 71 percent after 24 months beats the experience of its employer customers, insuring that employers save expense from reduced turnover. Self-development programs focus on accountability and personal empowerment. The ability to train a client to believe in himself and visualize a future is critical to success. TCR!'s personal empowerment program has been perfected and spun out as a separate profit center marketed and available to others in the workforce training field.

Twin Cities RISE! training programs focus on classwork and coaching in personal responsibility, conflict resolution, negotiation, and problem solving. Work skills include basic computer training, communication skills, critical thinking, customer service, and dealing with change and business growth. A coach is assigned to each participant throughout training, during the time the applicant seeks a full-time job, and during the entire first year of employment. Participants progress through the program in four or more ten-week phases and are committed to twelve to fifteen hours of training per week.

TCR! serves more than two thousand individuals in all of

its programs. It ranks as one of the largest job training providers for living-wage positions in the Twin Cities. Each participant signs a contract committing to one year of employment with a TCR! customer of their choosing at full wages and benefits. TCR! believes that its unique financial and skills-training model insures accountability and positive outcomes.

UJAMAA PLACE

This organization describes itself as serving "a lost generation of African American men who have lived many years in poverty without strong role models, have limited education, little or no real job experience, often involved in gang activity and have spent time in jail." In many cases these young men would spend the rest of their lives incarcerated without the services of organizations like Ujamaa Place.

Approximately fifty men are in the program at any given time. Of the forty who have completed the program, only one has re-offended. It is estimated that for the $5,000 to $10,000 invested in serving each client, roughly $50,000 is saved in public dollars for those who no longer re-offend. The transformation program includes five steps: finding stable housing, increasing educational skills, securing and retaining a job, connecting to family and children, and eliminating any ongoing involvement with the criminal justice system.

Educational support includes diagnostic testing accompanied by GED classes and individualized testing. Employment skills involve team building, quality communications, time management, accepting supervision, critical thinking and problem solving, financial and computer literacy, and internships. Life skills development includes navigating basic life systems, health consciousness, managing healthy relationships, engaging in children's lives, and defining black manhood and fatherhood.

Underlying goals of the program are to get men to think differently about themselves and believe in their own capabilities. The Ujamaa staff is African American and well equipped to relate one on one with their clients, who range in age from seventeen to thirty-one. Graduates of the program are maintaining stable housing, holding their jobs, or are enrolled in post-secondary education and job skill training programs. New initiatives at Ujamaa Place include securing additional funding to support expanded housing and employment training opportunities for their clients.

URBAN VENTURES LEADERSHIP FOUNDATION

Urban Ventures was formed in 1993 by Art Erickson to revitalize an area (Opportunity Zone, OZ) consisting of the six block area on either side of Lake Street between Second and Fourth Avenues in south Minneapolis. This area is the Urban Ventures campus. The key focus is on youth leadership, strengthening families, economic development, and creating meaningful work opportunities. Urban Ventures seeks to break the cycle of generational poverty in an area once dominated by crime, high unemployment, and hopelessness.

This area was economically robust in the 1940s and 1950s. The huge Sears complex on East Lake Street was the 1940s version of the Mall of America. People came from miles away to shop there. But in the course of time, and with the growth of the suburbs, the area deteriorated. In the 1960s Interstate Highways 94 and 35W divided the neighborhoods and displaced powerless people. As rail transport gave way to interstate trucking, local businesses such as car dealerships and farm equipment manufacturers moved to the suburbs. The rest of the primary economy—banks, retail, and services—followed.

Urban Ventures has been instrumental in helping revitalize the area. Today its key anchors are Wells Fargo Mortgage (located in the old Honeywell building), Abbott Northwestern Hospital, Children's Hospital, Hope Communities, and Project for Pride in Living offices and housing. The former Sears building has been converted into the Midtown Exchange, which has two million square feet of space for new businesses and housing units. Allina Health's executive offices have relocated there, along with the Midtown Global Market and Hennepin County Service Center.

Youth facilities include a recording studio, soccer fields, a high school, and small-scale retail for training and mentoring. Other services include a commercial-scale training kitchen, a food shelf, a clothing exchange, and a workforce training and referral center. Upward of two thousand men have passed through the Center for Fathering, an organization focused on re-educating fathers about their parental roles and potentially reuniting them with their children. KIX Field, the only regulation soccer field in the metro area, is used by Urban Stars programming to provide recreation for more than six hundred eager youth. In addition, Urban Ventures has youth participate in basketball and track and field programs that provide character building and teamwork experiences.

The new Cristo Rey Jesuit High School was built as part of the initiative to reverse the disappearance of such schools in the area; the number of high schools had dropped from seven to two. All of the first year's graduating class of sixty-one were accepted into college. This new school, with high academic standards and a welcoming learning environment, is dedicated to serving economically disadvantaged students. Part of the new experience at Cristo Rey is the Hire4Ed program, in which each student is required to work two days a week, thereby providing a supportive work experience as well as helping with tuition costs. The gym complex has four full-sized basketball courts. The walls are covered with the logos and messages from colleges and universities in the region to encourage students to plan for higher education.

Acknowledgements

For taking time to share with me their life stories I am so very grateful to the individuals who are included in this book. They have taken some risk in telling their stories. In many cases their struggle continues in terms of the racial, ethnic, social, and systems change barriers that must be overcome. Their enthusiasm and insights were inspiring. My thanks also to the leaders in our community from a broad range of non-profit organizations who identified them as star pupils.

Joe Nathan, who leads the Center for School Change, played a key role in mentoring David Ellis who went on to found the School for Recording Arts. Art Erickson, who co-founded Urban Ventures Leadership Foundation in south Minneapolis, made a life-long commitment to be there for John Turnipseed both before, during, and after his release from prison. Jim McCorkell, founder of College Possible, and his team were instrumental in inspiring and enabling both Pa Kong Lee and Cherkos Desalegn while still in high-school to prepare for and subsequently complete college. Pa Kong was born in Thailand and Cherkos in Ethiopia.

Jane Samrgia, executive director of HIRED, along with employment counselor Carie Yaeger, was responsible for connecting me with Ashley Bath and her remarkable story of overcoming extreme abuse and neglect. Jeff Washburne, director of the City of Lakes Land Trust, enabled the refugee we named Mario Owusu, from Sudan in Africa, to purchase an affordable home and settle his family in north Minneapolis. I am grateful to Paul Fate, former executive director of Common Bond

Communities, and his colleagues Ann Ruff and Debra Lande, manager of Common Bond's Advantage Center Teen Program, for selecting Bibi Abdalla, whose family immigrated from Somalia, as one whose story should be included in the book.

The remarkable story of Beth Milbrant's transition from federal prison to living wage employment was made possible by Steve Shedivy, director of marketing for Summit Academy OIC, and Catherine Olson, executive assistant to their president and CEO Louis King. The narrative of another successful graduate of our criminal justice system, Lante Morris, came from a referral by Steve Thomas, former executive director of the Network for Better Futures, an innovative rehabilitation program for ex-offenders. Melissa Carr is the alumnae services coordinator for the Jeremiah Program, which has helped many of the region's single moms find both shelter and the needed education skills to gain a living wage job. She brought the remarkable story of Tiffany Meeks to my attention. Shegitu Kebede's difficult and long journey from Ethiopia to Kenya and finally to the United States illustrates an amazing triumph of the human sprit over evil. Joseph Selvaggio, who has founded several of our leading non-profit organizations and currently heads Micro Grants, introduced me to Shegitu over lunch at the restaurant she founded called Flamingo, located on Syndicate Street and University Avenue in St. Paul.

Todd Otis has championed the cause of early childhood education for more than two decades. He currently serves as chief advancement officer and senior vice president of Think Small, an early childhood advocacy and support organization. It was Todd who identified Kandy McDonal as one who could best describe the challenges faced by single moms in attempting to navigate our welfare support and early childhood education systems. Ibro and Mary Tobacovic's narrow escape from ethnic cleansing in Bosnia is a tribute to their local countrymen who put their own careers and lives at risk. It was because of his long-time friendship with University of Minnesota professor Larry Miller and subsequent support from colleagues John and Sonia Cairns that I met Ibro and Mary.

David Nasby, retired vice president of the General Mills Foundation, was executive director of the City, Inc, a youth alternative school and drop-in center, when John Pacheco was in high school. Over lunch he and wife Karen enthusiastically suggested that John's story be included in the book. St. Paul banker Bill Sands invited several of us to visit Ujama Place, a rehabilitation program for hardened ex-offenders. There we met Kadar Hickman, program manager and education director, who urged me to meet with Raymond Jackson and record his tragic story of abuse and neglect.

I am especially grateful to my wife Anne who has introduced me to many of the non-profit leaders mentioned in the book. Her work over many years has been focussed in the areas of affordable housing, education, combatting racism and poverty, improving the criminal justice system, job skill training, public affairs consulting and fostering greater international understanding of the issues impacting third world countries.

Mike Huck of the Greater Twin Cities United Way and my colleague at Urban Adventure, was with me from the start, helping advise on the content of the book. Also my thanks to editor John Toren whose careful attention to detail, structure, and design, has greatly enhanced the quality of this text. One of Minnesota's hidden treasures is my publisher, Norton Stillman of Nodin Press, who continues to promote and support a wide range of Minnesota authors.

ABOUT THE AUTHOR

A Minneapolis native, Peter Heegaard began his business career in 1960 with the Trust Investment Group of Northwestern National Bank of Minneapolis, which he headed from 1980 to 1986. He was founder and Managing Principal of Lowry Hill, an investment subsidiary of Wells Fargo. He retired March 31, 1996, to serve as consultant and community volunteer to several foundations and non-profit organizations. In 1997 he founded Urban Adventure, a Twin Cities based educational program that has exposed more than three hundred leaders in business to our most challenging urban issues. His book *Heroes Among Us* was published in September 2008. It covers the lives of eleven Minnesota social entrepreneurs who founded many of the leading regional non-profit organizations. A second book, *More Bang for Your Buck*, calculates the economic value of community based programs. In June of 2010 he was awarded the degree of Doctor of Humane Letters from Augsburg College. He currently chairs the board of the Philips Eye Institute Foundation. Past board service includes: Board of Pensions Presbyterian Church USA, The Minneapolis Foundation, Charles K. Blandin Foundation, Hennepin County Library, Citizens League, Legal Rights Center, Presbyterian Homes Minnesota, Ready 4K, Van Dusen Air Inc., M.A. Gedney Company and trustee of Macalester College. Heegaard is a member of Plymouth Congregational Church and a former member of St. Luke Presbyterian Church where he served as Elder. He is a graduate of Dartmouth College and the Amos Tuck School of Business Administration. His favorite pastimes include fly fishing, hiking, cross country skiing, and biking. Heegaard lives with his wife, Anne, in Minneapolis. They have three children and eight grandchildren.